T0374972

Outward Odyssey
A People's History of Spaceflight

Series editor
Colin Burgess

The Light of
Earth

Reflections on a Life in Space

Al Worden with Francis French

Foreword by Dee O'Hara

UNIVERSITY OF NEBRASKA PRESS • LINCOLN

Library of Congress Cataloging-in-
Publication Data
Names: Worden, Al, 1932–2020, author. |
French, Francis, author.
Title: The light of Earth: reflections on
a life in space / Al Worden, with Francis
French; foreword by Dee O'Hara.
Description: Lincoln: University of
Nebraska Press, [2021] | Series: Outward
odyssey: a people's history of spaceflight |
Includes index.
Identifiers: LCCN 2021007087
ISBN 9781496228659 (hardback)
ISBN 9781496229632 (epub)
ISBN 9781496229649 (pdf)
Subjects: LCSH: Worden, Al, 1932–2020. |
Astronauts—United States—Biography. |
Manned space flight—United States—
History. | Project Apollo (U.S.)
Classification: LCC TL789.85.W67 A3
2021 | DDC 629.450092 [B]—dc23
LC record available at
https://lccn.loc.gov/2021007087

Set in Garamond Premier Pro by
Mikala R. Kolander.

Contents

Illustrations

Foreword

I first met Al Worden in 1966 when he arrived at NASA in Houston following his selection as an astronaut. He introduced himself, turned in his air force medical records, and stayed for a brief chat. I thought, "Gee, what a nice guy!" It turned out my first impression was right. Fifty-four years later, Al was *still* a nice guy.

It was my job to medically check out every astronaut on the day they launched into space. I did it from 1961's first U.S. mission, flown by Alan Shepard, to 1981's first space shuttle flight. I was thrilled when, one morning in 1971, I helped Al prepare for the ride of a lifetime. To go to the moon was a goal he had worked so hard for, and he carried it out with humor, dedication to the job, and a poet's eye that went far beyond his job description.

Following his *Apollo 15* mission, he moved out to NASA's Ames Research Center, located in California's Bay Area. He became the chief of the Systems Division, enjoyed his new job, and began really enjoying California life. He was very well liked and respected; the Ames Center management was really pleased to have him serving on the center's management staff.

He was such a kind, nice guy that when I chose to do the same thing and transfer to Ames the following year, he volunteered to fly to Houston and then drive me and my goofy dog, Jacques, out to California. The drive out was an adventure, to say the least. It was during the middle of the gas crisis, so we endured long lines to fill up—and Al endured my dog. He teased me about that dog for the rest of his life.

How do you summarize someone who lived as rich and varied a life as Al? I can only break it down into some key words.

Courage: It takes courage to be a jet pilot and an astronaut. Not everyone could do it.

Perseverance: He had this in spades. To leave his job in Texas and forge ahead with a new career was brave—he didn't give up.

Gregarious: I am not sure he ever met a stranger.

Fun loving: He was always ready with a laugh and ready for a party.

Friend: He was a very good friend; driving someone with a dog to California proved that.

I was very sad when I heard that Al was no longer with us. I would see him at space events at least once a year, and I always looked forward to the moment I'd hear his distinctive laugh. I will miss him greatly. Thank goodness his friend and coauthor Francis French had completed this book project with him. Al had so many insights to share with the world, and now, with this book, he will continue to do so.

Dee O'Hara
Astronauts' nurse

The Light of Earth

1

The Unmaking of an Ex-Astronaut

It turns out that there is no such thing as an ex-astronaut.

Sure, we can retire from NASA and spend years doing other things. But it's not our choice whether we are still considered an astronaut. It seems that other people get to decide that.

When my generation of astronauts retired from NASA one by one, we generally tried to leave the astronaut stuff behind for a while. It's not too surprising. We'd all been type A personalities, at the top of whatever career we'd chosen to pursue. We weren't the kind to rest on prior accomplishments. Whatever we picked to do next—mostly working in the business world—we wanted to be the best at that too. We shook the space program off and moved forward. There wasn't much choice anyway; in the mid- to late 1970s, no one cared about Apollo much anymore. Many of us grew our hair long, grew a mustache or even a beard, dressed much less conservatively, and went with the times. For a while you'd never have been able to place us if you'd tried to spot us by looking at old NASA photos. Our different directions in life also meant we rarely met in anything other than small groups.

But now, when I go to space events, we're all back in the same room again like some perennial high school reunion. Those of us who still have hair now generally have it cut short, NASA style. And although the closest we've been to a jet that week was probably flying in the dreaded middle seat of a commercial flight, we're all wearing NASA flight jackets. We even have military-looking name tags and an American flag on the shoulder—in case we forget our names and where we're from, I guess. We're back in uniform. We're each dressed as "the astronaut" again.

I'm a lot prouder of the non-NASA stuff that I did in my life. NASA was all about learning a skill. Running for Congress, starting my own company, heading a charitable organization—those were individual achievements of mine. Nevertheless, I'm back to wearing that flight jacket. Ironically, I had to have one made. My old ones were long gone.

People think of Apollo astronauts like some band of brothers with a shared experience. But there's a difference between us and, let's say, your typical World War II fighter squadron. In that squadron, you've all gone through hell together. You've protected the people with you. If you were the wingman, you protected the lead, and if you were the lead, you protected the wingman. You flew together, you fought together, and some members died together. But with the Apollo program, everybody was an individual. We never all flew together, so there is a big difference in mentality. Fifty years later, of course, we get back together, and it's kind of fun, and we reminisce about old things. But I reminisce about things that basically didn't have that much to do with the program. For example, astronaut Paul Weitz was probably my best friend in that whole group. When I saw him, Paul and I talked about fishing. Then when he lost his wife, which was a huge blow for him, I helped talk him through that. It's not about space exploration. It's personal stuff. It's catching up with old friends.

You know those big sixties rock bands who break up with differences that can never be reconciled—until they get back together and tour a few decades later? I think what's happening with us is similar. All those things that caused stress and distress have disappeared into history. They're gone. What's left over is that we all have something in common that we did. Whether good or bad, whether we liked it fifty years ago or not, those things are all historic now, and there's no reason to cry over spilled milk. But I do have a few exceptions. I separate out those who were good people and those who did me damage. Some of the damage that was done to me, I can't forgive.

It's a weird thought to have, but you know, sometimes when I am saying a quick goodbye to these guys in some hotel lobby, or at the end of a banquet, or at the airport, I know it's the last time I might see them. Because that has happened so many times before with old colleagues. Do I tell them they were important to me? That I am grateful they were in my life? Or do they already know?

There was one guy whom I was particularly glad to have the opportunity to say something like that to—my fellow astronaut Dick Gordon. I worried about Dick. He had a huge load on his shoulders, taking care of his late wife, and it aged him rapidly. Once she passed away, I wasn't sure how long he would last. It's like he had a duty to perform, and he was going to keep doing that and not give up. He was pretty tied to her. That again was a deep personal connection that had no real connection to the space program, other than that was where we'd met.

So being an astronaut doesn't define me. That's not how I see myself.

When giving talks to the public, I used to talk about my flight to the moon because I wanted to talk about the flight. Now I talk about it because I want to motivate people to do something else. So I use the experience as a tool. The jacket is a tool too. It is all public perception. If people see me in the jacket, they say, "Oh, I know who you are, and if you're going to give a talk, I'm going to come and listen."

I think I've developed a persona who people really enjoy listening to. I don't pat myself on the back. I've found a niche out there where I am not promoting myself—I'm promoting something else, such as STEM education. Such as following your dreams. Such as how to organize a business. But I have to wear that jacket, because that's the thing that attracts people to begin with— then they listen to my message.

The last big tour I did in Europe, I went everywhere. But I particularly liked the Swiss events that I did, because I talked to high school kids. I had a gymnasium filled with hundreds of students, and you could have heard a pin drop. It was wonderful, because I really had them. I was *really* talking to them.

I do my talks a little differently than most astronauts. When I can, I talk from the floor; I don't get up on stage. I always feel that if you're talking from the stage, you're lecturing. Up on a stage, you have spotlights on you; you don't see the audience. If you are talking from the floor, you're just talking to them personally. That makes a huge difference in the way people perceive you and how you get along with them. The closer you are to an audience, the more eye contact you make, and the better it is for everybody. I learned over the years that becoming part of the audience, while giving my story to them, is really important. That's when they really listen.

I'm also the only Apollo astronaut still giving talks at the Kennedy Space Center. Every other astronaut who speaks there flew in later programs. And I'll be very honest with you—I like to do it because it keeps my feet on the ground. I think it's healthy for me.

There are some astronauts who may have a cause to promote, but they're more interested in talking about what wonderful things they did in the past.

They might tie it in to some future space direction they advocate for. That is fine. But they are mostly big on selling themselves as the person who went to the moon. That's a promotion thing. I have a hard time with that; it's just not something that I'd want to do.

Some astronauts are so big on pushing their own pet projects that when I run into them in a lobby somewhere, they immediately start pitching. They are so focused that they forget their audience. I usually already know that they've been out there advocating. And either I'm already on board, or I couldn't care less. Either way, I'm not really listening.

I'm much more interested in what the general public want to ask me about.

Probably the most common question I get is, "What's it like in space?" There's no good answer to that. When I talk about being in space, first off, I have to correct a misconception that people have about what we call zero-g. There's no such thing as zero-g, so that's confusing. I have to explain that, in space, we were, in fact, in free fall the whole time. If you're in orbit around Earth, you're in free fall, but you're going forward fast enough that you never fall back to Earth.

So once I go through that quickly for people, I explain that being in space means not only that you are in free fall but also that the spacecraft you're inside is in free fall. So you can move around up or down, sideways or whatever you want to do inside there, because you and the spacecraft are both falling at the same speed. It's like there's no gravity on you, even though there is. That's very confusing to people.

I then explain that if you really want to know what it's like to be inside that can, in free fall, moving around—it's a little like being underwater. Do you know how to swim? Can you swim underwater? Now imagine that there's no water. You're just in a void. You can flap your arms all you want, but you're not going to go anywhere. If you're in the water, you can paddle around. But without any water around you, you're not going to move. You have to touch something and push off to move around. That's what it's like being in space. That's my answer to that.

I've also had questions such as, "What was it like during launch?" and, "What were you thinking during launch?" And this is where I really get people.

"I wasn't thinking about anything."

"Were you scared?"

"No."

"Why not?"

"Either we're going to make it, or we're not. If we don't make it, we'll be in the history books; if we make it, we're heroes."

They're not expecting that.

Then there's always the standard question about going to the bathroom and that kind of stuff, but that's been answered by just about every astronaut, I think.

What are people trying to get from our conversation? Are they trying to get an experience that they can never have, or are they trying to understand mine?

I really don't think most adults care to understand. Little kids do not have this problem. They'll ask whatever they want. And they want to know the answer. Adults, in my opinion, very often ask a question just to get a little closer to me. To show me that they know a little bit about what happened in my life, and then perhaps I'll be a friend to them or something. They don't really want an answer so much as they want familiarity. A connection.

What I find interesting is that the more knowledgeable somebody is about spaceflight, the better the question. They have studied and come to the conclusion that there's something about a part of spaceflight that they don't understand. So they'll ask a question about it—and they want to know the answer. Because it fills in something in their brain, something missing in their knowledge.

Here's an example. I'm not a fan of Hillary Clinton politically, but I will tell you this. In 1994 my wife Jill and I went to the White House for the twenty-fifth anniversary of *Apollo 11*. As we headed into the reception, the First Lady was the first one in line. She talked to Jill, and then she talked to me and asked me a question. And she stared me right in the eye while I was answering. She wanted to know what I had to say. We got to Bill, who threw off a question—I mean, just a nothing question—and he never looked me in the eye. He was surveying the room while I answered. I thought, "Well, you prick. You don't need an answer. This is just something you do. You don't care." There's the difference between the two of them. That's why Hillary has that connection and he doesn't. He's a very charismatic guy, but he's not very focused.

I run into both kinds of people a lot. I wonder why some even bother to ask. If it's in a big crowd, I think it's because they get the stage for a minute. "Gee, I need to stand up in front of these five hundred people and ask a question. Maybe I know the answer, and maybe I don't. And I don't give a rat's ass what the answer is, but I want to get up. Then everybody will see me. They'll hear my question, and it'll make me better or something." I don't know. But I think a lot of people ask questions for that reason. They want other people around to think, "Hey, there's a guy who knows what he's talking about."

I don't think there are any dumb questions. I always answer a question, even if it seems silly. I think there may be questions where the questioner doesn't know what they're talking about, but the questions are always something that I can answer. In my opinion there's no such thing as a silly question when it comes to space. There are so many facets to it, and a thousand things you could ask. I've probably heard them all, although I may hear one question one time and another question five hundred times. There's always a grain of reality in the question, and it probably needs to be answered. I might answer the question in a different way because the questioner didn't phrase it properly, to get it back on track. But I just don't know of any really dumb questions. Eating in space, going to the bathroom in space—a lot of people think they are silly questions, but they're not. Those are vital, and as we get into longer and longer flights, such as going to Mars, which is going to take a year and a half, those questions are going to come back around again. We're going to have to deal with them in some way.

Actually, thinking about it more, there is one kind of question I think is dumb. When I was asked by a reporter, "Who are you, and what did you do?" I looked at them and replied, "You're interviewing me, and you don't even know who I am? That's pretty silly." So that was a dumb question. I do a lot of TV interviews where they're not really that well prepared, and they want me to repeat my whole history and what I've done, because they never checked it out beforehand. They had a call from their boss, who said, "I want you to go to this place here and interview Al Worden. Right now. He was on *Apollo 15*. He's been to the moon." That's all they know when they see me. So they do start asking some pretty asinine questions.

Other ways that I relate to people have changed over the decades. At one time, everybody wanted an autograph. Many still do. But now it seems everybody wants a photo with me. It has become the equivalent—almost a bigger thing. And people can get a photograph for free. Autographs might cost something. At one time, a camera and film were expensive. Now, everyone has a cell phone.

And people take advantage of autographs too. When I give talks at the

Kennedy Space Center, part of the deal is that I also go to the enormous Space Shop on site and sign autographs for the public. We're supposed to just sit and sign, for no charge. I can't tell you how many times I've had collectors come in there with a whole stack of stuff in their arms for me to sign, just for their personal collection—or worse, to sell online right away. A collector bringing their own stuff for me to sign doesn't help the Space Shop at all. The whole idea of me signing is to help the store. This became a pet peeve of mine and something I had to rectify. So now we have a rule. If they buy something in the store, then I'll sign it. Happily. Otherwise, no.

That might sound a little mean. But you have to understand—after so many decades signing autographs, I have seen every trick in the book. Not long ago, someone emailed me and asked me to sign multiple baseballs. I kept putting him off. And then one day, I walked out of my home—in a gated community— and he was standing in front of me. I don't know how he got in, and I don't know where he got my home address. I signed them all just to get rid of him. And then he contacted me again and wanted more. I told him if he wanted any more, he should come to an autograph show. With experiences such as that, the joy of giving an autograph every time is gone.

Even a small number of the well-meaning collectors who come to auto- graph shows don't really interact with me as a human being. They have a col- lectible they want signed in a certain place, in a certain way, with a certain pen, and I'm just a machine. I'm the thing that makes that happen. There's no eye contact. Thankfully, that's pretty rare, because most folks who come to those autograph shows are excited, happy, cheerful people who brighten my day. Many have become friends. These are the people for whom it still feels special to me. If someone brings up a poster of the crescent Earth photo I took, then I know that that person has thought about it. It's something they want. Then I'll sign it with great care. I'll probably even tell them about the amazing experience of taking the shot.

But the people I am not so keen on—I get a little short with them. If I think somebody is using me or I think somebody is asking for too much or stuffing something under my nose without being very nice about it, then I will very quickly sign, and I'm done.

I have a similar rationale at the Space Shop. Here's my thinking process: If somebody buys something that's of value at the store, then I'll write, "Al Worden, *Apollo 15*." If it's a book I wrote, I'll ask their name and write that, plus, "Best Wishes." Until I started the new policy of just store items, if it was just a map of the visitor's center, which they got for free, then I just wrote, "Al Worden." A lot of people wanted me to sign their entrance ticket. Well, that's not something they bought at the Space Shop. But I'd just sign, "Al Worden," on it. I didn't put my flight on that. I mean, they could have bought a postcard for fifty cents and gotten a signature on it. Bought a T-shirt or a hat. Instead of throwing a napkin at me.

The rude behavior has, unfortunately, been a part of my life for decades. I still remember one of our *Apollo 15* postflight tours in 1971 where the three of us were up at a table on a long stage, having lunch. I believe it was in Chicago. Lunch was chicken. Without fail, every lunch was chicken. I had a piece on a fork, and I got it about halfway to my mouth. A woman came up to the table, grabbed my hand, and put it back on the plate. "I want you to sign this," she said. "You can't eat—sign that autograph before you eat." I looked at her, and you can imagine what names I was calling her in my head. But what was I going to do? I mean, I was up there in front of five hundred people, and as rude as she was . . . well, I said, "Uh—okay."

I've also heard some Americans say, "I paid taxes so you could fly to the moon. You owe me an autograph." But folks today didn't pay for me. So you know—stuff it. I believe there was a certain sense of responsibility I had to the public around the time of the flight, because we flew at taxpayer expense. However, there is a limit to that, and over fifty years of being an astronaut is definitely way beyond that limit.

Once I became a private citizen, I got selective about free things. I do a lot of charity events with that in mind. I don't owe anybody for anything, and I resent those who demand something because "we paid for your trip." That is one reason I got so involved with charities, such as the Astronaut Scholarship Foundation and, more recently, the Astronaut Al Worden Endeavour Scholarship. I'm going to continue to use my astronaut title as a tool to raise money for a new generation of engineers, scientists, and explorers for as long as I can.

So just because I am wearing that jacket again, it doesn't mean I owe you anything. If I've ever met you and I was nice to you, it's because I truly wanted to be and I was glad to meet you.

2

Doing Well

The sixties were a huge time of transformational change in America. And like most astronauts, I missed out on nearly all of it.

We were too doggone busy to pay much attention to that kind of stuff. I was engrossed in astronaut training, doing the engineering that we needed to do, studying geology, making field trips—endless stuff. I don't recall even reading a newspaper back then. Not only did I not have time; I didn't have the concern, either. I didn't care. We were on a path, and we stuck to it and did what had to be done.

By 1973 life was as different as it could get. I was living close to San Francisco, with long hair and a big mustache, wearing suede jackets and dating some really interesting women. One of my friends was the music critic for the *San Francisco Chronicle*, and I used to hang around with him a lot. He'd have a party when the music groups came to town. He'd call and say, "Come on down," so I'd drive into the city and party with all kinds of musicians, actors, people like that—folks such as John Denver, Sammy Davis Jr., and Glen Campbell. Actresses and heiresses. It was a fascinating scene.

I'd been a Michigan farm boy, attended the military academy, and was—technically—still in the U.S. Air Force. This was a different world. But by then I'd had so many different experiences in my life. I'd lived and worked in different places, with different people, both in this country and overseas. That Michigan farm boy was long gone. I don't think there's much of that farm boy left today.

I love San Francisco. It's a great town. At least, it was; I don't know what it is like today. I know it's probably the most expensive city in the country right now. Things were fairly loose then. Associations were pretty free, and people were not inhibited in any way. Everyone was easygoing and open. It made for some great times.

What I remember about San Francisco back then are the gay men. I'm not gay, but I'd go into the gay bars. I never met anyone there whom I didn't like—they were all really nice, just living their lives. I was dating a girl out there at the time, and when I didn't take her to dinner on a Saturday night, she would call a couple of her gay male friends to take her out instead.

I asked, "Why do you do that?"

"Because they're the best! They know their food, they know their wine, they know how to dance and how to treat me well, and they're not going to put a hand on me. So I am perfectly safe with them, and I have a great time."

It was a very friendly city. When I had the time, I would drive in to San Francisco to have dinner, go to the park, or just hang out. It was especially nice when my daughters were visiting.

San Francisco was very laid-back, very casual; there was a big crowd up in Haight-Ashbury who were still doing the hippie thing. The poet laureate of San Francisco and I became friends, and we did poetry readings together at a bar downtown. We'd go back to his house up in Haight-Ashbury and have coffee. Haight-Ashbury was really the flower power capital of San Francisco back then. Everybody was cool with everybody.

I used to have lunch with George Moscone, who later became the mayor of San Francisco. I loved to go to Ghirardelli Square on Sundays and watch the kites, the jugglers, singers, actors, and other street performers. It was magical. I'd just sit and watch people walking around and then have dinner at the Chinese restaurant there. I always considered January to be the best month in San Francisco. The skies were clear, and the days were warm. Just south of there, it got really cold—but the city itself, for some reason, always seemed to be really nice in January. I really enjoyed it. But I knew that my time there was coming to an end, and I had to figure out what I was going to do the rest of my life.

All the hard work I had put in over the years in my life had come to naught. I'd been fired as an astronaut over a scandal involving postal covers taken to the moon. I'd been ordered to get out of Houston. I'd been told unofficially that I would never get promoted in the air force again, something that turned out to be untrue. I was only still working for NASA because I had found somewhere to hide for a while. In the decades since then, the *Apollo 15* flight has become more and more important to the people who matter. And almost everybody I talk to today says, "You got screwed back then." But that's not how I felt at the time. I was at rock bottom. My marriage had ended. My kids were in another state. My astronaut career had been killed. I was so discouraged when I went out to California that I just let it all go. Letting my hair and that mustache grow was getting into the culture of the San Francisco scene, at least for a few years. I even had a book of my poetry published. This phase of my life didn't last long, but it was a reaction to what had happened to me. Kind of my dismissal, I guess, of what had been done to me.

When I got that call from Deke Slayton, the director of Flight Operations, and was told that I was no longer needed, I was like an outcast. Guys whom I knew really, really well suddenly became—different. It's not that they weren't friendly. It's that everybody let me know, "We don't want to be too close to you." They did it to protect their careers, but more than anything, they also did it to let me know that I had let them down. I was the most miserable guy you can imagine back then.

I didn't have a very good job at first. I was in a little office inside a hangar, and it was not much fun. But I think this drove me to pay more attention to what was going on outside. So I got to know people. I learned a lot. For example, I learned that the worst thing you can do is be in a hot tub and drink wine, because it really gets to you.

I had been so structured and so disciplined before and during *Apollo 15*. So going out to NASA's Ames Research Center—and the way I went out—kind of destroyed all that. I said to myself, "Ah, screw it—I'm just going to do whatever I want to do." And before long, I enjoyed Ames. After my initial stretch, I was given a good job out there. The people at Ames were a very different crowd than the folks in Houston. Many of the Ames researchers wore long white lab coats and had mustaches and beards. When I'd see them all walking down the street to go to lunch, I'd think, "God, this looks like a science fiction movie." And when they were not in their white lab coats, they were pretty, uh, loose. Back in Houston the NASA folks still had buzz cuts, pocket protectors, and white shirts. They were uptight. They didn't know what was going on outside Houston. The Ames folks were all very smart scientists and researchers, searching for life out in the universe, doing long-term bed rest studies, and making space suits. They had a few airplanes to fly as part of the airborne science group, including a couple of U-2s. There was some interesting stuff going on out there, and a lot of it had very little to do with space.

I had to go to New York one time, and so I called George H. W. Bush. He was ambassador to the United Nations at the time, and I knew him from our *Apollo 15* postflight tour. He said, "Well, we've got to have lunch." So I told him where I was staying, and he said, "I'll be out in front to pick you up." At the appointed time, a big black limousine showed up, and there was George in the back, smoking a big cigar. I got in, and we went to some very fancy New York club. It was a very formal place, and I was wearing a suede jacket over a turtleneck sweater. They wouldn't let us in unless I was wearing a coat and tie. New York was pretty straitlaced like that. That really annoyed George—he wasn't annoyed at me, but at them. So we went to some public restaurant instead, where it didn't make a difference.

I used to drive over the mountains to Santa Cruz a lot and then down through the endless fields of artichokes on the Monterey peninsula. It was just very comfortable country back then. I looked at buying some land down in Saratoga, by the south end of San Francisco Bay, before you get up into the Redwoods. Saratoga was an interesting little throwback place, an old western town. In fact, to go shopping, you walked along a plank sidewalk. Pretty land around there. My God, it was gorgeous land. I was going to turn the western side of thirty acres, draped over the top of a hill, into a vineyard. It would have been good for that. But I never got around to it.

I was really just riding out the storm there. I wanted to leave the air force with some dignity—plus, more importantly, the full pension I would earn if I worked for just a couple of more years. I got to a point at Ames where I was comfortable with what I was doing and comfortable with working for the government. But at the same time, I had such a bad taste in my mouth about what had happened that I decided I wasn't going to stick around. So when I got my twenty years in, I retired. I left NASA and the air force in 1975 knowing I did not want to go work for a big company. As a matter of fact, feeling kind of tainted from the end of my NASA career, I wasn't sure any big company would want me on board anyway.

So I never really tried. And at the same time, I thought, "I've had enough of the big corporate businesses on my back; I think I'm going to strike out on my own and do whatever." And that's what I did. So I loaded all my belongings into a motor home and hitched my sports car to the back of it. I headed east and went back to school. Living in a motor home in winter is cold, but I made it work. Life wasn't going to keep me down for long.

It makes me think about the kids I went to school with back in Jackson, Michigan. In retrospect, I think I could see who was going to make it out of there and who wasn't. It would be interesting to go back and confirm what happened to all of them and to see if my observations were correct.

I'd realized that if I didn't go to college, if I stayed in my hometown, I was going to be relegated to working my way up in a company somewhere, starting out on the assembly line. In fact, one summer, when I was still in high school, I worked for a company named Handley-Brown, which made domestic water heaters. I ran the big machine that formed the metal into the cylinder that would then be welded to make the heater. I used to think then, "This can't be the rest of my life. I'm not going to get stuck here. This is not for me." I had bigger aspirations than that. I couldn't accept that.

The kids I went to school with came from all walks of life. Some came from poor families; some, from families of doctors and lawyers. What none of us realized at the time was that once we got out of high school and went to college, we were on our own. So it's not what your parents can do for you that puts you in a different category from everybody else at school. It's what you have to do yourself for the rest of your life. You've got to make your own way. You cannot live on your parents' finances all your life. So many of the kids who came from poor families did much better later in life than those from rich families. Why? Because they knew what it was like to not have money. They had a motivation to do things. In fact, the class clown at my school, whom everybody laughed at, became the most successful guy in my class. He became the president of a number of companies. He'd come from a poor family, but he worked his way up. One guy whom I was in a band with in high school was from the wrong side of the tracks, but he wrote music, played until he was very, very good, and worked his way through college teaching the accordion. He went to medical school and became a very successful cardiac surgeon.

I think sometimes a person's better off really applying themselves to learning a trade and business, such as construction, instead of going to college. What happens to kids who go to college? So many of them just go to work for a big corporation, and they never break that door open where they become entrepreneurs. Some of them do, but I think the vast majority become engineers, technicians, and accountants, in a bureaucracy where they have to work their way up within the organization. So I'm not sure that college is always the solution. I think it depends on the individual. If you are very aggressive and very entrepreneurial, going to college gives you the tools to be successful. But I think you can also learn them without going to college if you really apply yourself to what you're doing. Learning a trade from the bottom up can be much more beneficial.

When you're eighteen and out of high school, if you start in a career such as building homes, you have nothing to lose. And so you take every risk and every chance there is. You're successful, or you're not. But if you are successful, man, the sky's the limit. And I think that's what happens to some kids. Look at most successful entrepreneurs, and my guess is that a big percentage of them never went to college. One exception is the software, programming-type people; you have to have some good education to do that. But in basic industries—plumbing, electrical, home building, automotive, all those kinds of things—you learn on the job, and you apply yourself to it.

I think that kids who grew up in families where they had to work to get along were better off in the long run. Now, some of them took the easy road and got a job that needed no qualifications. I know a lot of my classmates did that. They worked in local companies back home, such as becoming guards at the local prison and that kind of thing. They didn't really go any further. I think a lot of that was caused by the kind of family they grew up in. My mother was very interested in us all going on to further education. She couldn't pay for us, but she encouraged us. Only two of us did—my brother Jerry and I. We both put ourselves through college. My brother Jim was kind of a lost child for a long time, but when he got his act together, he became a pilot, eventually becoming a corporate pilot and having a very nice life.

In general, I think the answer to what you do with your life is hard work and dedication and not expecting somebody else to do it for you. I have a real problem when people just assume that somebody else ought to help them. I have seen that particularly with kids who are descendants of very wealthy people. All too often, they sit around waiting for their folks to die so that they can get their parents' money. They're not going to do it on their own. I often think that if you get too much given to you when you're young, you lose the edge—you lose the motivation to really put yourself out there to get something. I think it's all a question of expectations. It sounds cliché, but there's no substitute for hard work.

When I left Michigan and went to the U.S. Military Academy at West Point, I wondered how I was going to survive. The first year of military life was brutal. But I soon realized that if I kept my head down and worked hard, people noticed. I never promoted myself. I did the best I could, and it became a routine.

When I then joined the air force and was selected to go to the Empire Test

Pilot School in England, it was exactly the same. I saw that the quiet, competent guy will be the one who gets noticed. You're always there, always ready to do whatever they ask you to do. Always ready to go someplace and do whatever needs to be done. I realized that my engineering background really fit well with my flying ability, and so I did very well at the ETPS. I graduated second in the class. The guy who came first was an Englishman, and I figured there was no way that was not going to happen!

That same thing happened when I got into the Astronaut Office. When we first got there, we were in classes for most of our first year, being taught by some of our support team. A couple of us decided that we could do better, so we went to Al Shepard, our boss, and said, "Hey, you know, we can do a better job than those guys." He said, "Okay, go ahead and do it." So we ended up teaching. It wasn't because we wanted to make an issue of how good we were. It was because we could do better. That was the attitude I had throughout the whole thing. I never tried to push myself, but I wanted to make sure that I did the right thing and that people understood that I was doing the right thing. You do not brownnose; you do not sidle up to the managers and try to be their best friends, because in the long run, that's not going to do you any good. I thought that trying to cozy up to the management was probably the worst thing we could do. Just show how good you are. That's the important thing.

That does not mean the Astronaut Office wasn't fiercely competitive. By and large, all the guys—at least my group of guys selected—were striving to beat the pack. We were on the homestretch, and we could see the finish line ahead. We started out in a big group. Then somebody got a little bit ahead, and we could see the shuffling.

Most of the guys I knew who got into the program were type A personalities. They were aggressive individuals who were not going to sit back and wait for anybody. They were going to go out and do their thing. When we got into the program, it was pretty clear that certain people were going to make flights and certain people weren't. There was a big internal push inside each of us, I think, that said, "I've got to get myself into a position where I can make a flight. How do I approach this thing to do that?" Whatever job I got, man, I really went after it 1,000 percent. And I was one of the very first guys in my group to fly. I believe I was also jointly the first to be assigned, working on *Apollo 9*, which soon turned into a backup crew position for *Apollo 12*.

In some work environments, brownnosing is the only way to get ahead. But even if I had come to the conclusion that the way to get an advantage and to get a flight was to go for a drink every night with my other boss, Deke Slayton, I still wouldn't have done it. That was not me. I have never promoted myself that way. I wanted to do the things that I was good at doing and qualified to do, not because I knew somebody, but because I was good enough. That's been my attitude my whole life, even on the farm. You can go back to the time I was twelve years old and was self-sufficient, doing my own thing. I didn't need anybody else; I wasn't dependent on anybody.

As time goes by, history doesn't change, but it takes on a different aura. When I went to Ames, the folks in Houston were looking at me as a culprit who deserved to be fired. By the time my book *Falling to Earth* came out on the fortieth anniversary of my moonflight, there was enough evidence along the way to show that even though I was part of what happened, I was also a victim of it. My *Apollo 15* crewmate Jim Irwin and I weren't innocent. But we had been sucked in by a guy we really trusted, who to this day has never taken responsibility. When the book came out, people read the full story for the very first time. They finally understood that maybe the fingers were pointed in the wrong direction back in 1972.

My coauthor, Francis, was with me signing books at the book-launch events in the Smithsonian Air and Space Museum in Washington DC. It turned out that Francis also had some business that week with Charlie Bolden, the former space shuttle astronaut who was now the NASA administrator. One evening, Francis and I went out for a great meal with Charlie and his wife, Jackie. It was a wonderful night of storytelling and laughter.

Charlie had been a friend of mine for many years, so I didn't really put any special significance on it. But the next day, Francis pointed out the symbolism. Decades earlier, I'd been kicked out of Houston. Now, the venerable Smithsonian Institution was publishing my book, my reputation was restored, and the head of NASA was taking me out to dinner. It was a complete turnaround from forty years earlier.

I wouldn't say it completely closed the chapter on what had happened to me. But there is a sense of redemption I've had, in the years since, that has been very meaningful. Hard work will get you many places in life. Sometimes, despite all that work, the world can hit you with a crushing blow. But if you don't let it stop you—at least, not for long—and you continue with dignity and honor, the truth has a way of coming out. Despite everything, I'm very happy with where I have ended up. There's a lot more I want to do, and I'm not done yet.

3

Enemies to Allies

When the space race with the Soviet Union began in 1957, I was ready to give my life to stop them.

I wasn't in the space program—not yet. I was flying jets in the air force during that tense part of the Cold War, as part of an interceptor squadron defending the nation's capital. If the Russians sent in bombers armed with nuclear weapons, my job was to knock them out of the sky before they could get anywhere near the shore. Thankfully, nothing like that ever happened. The Soviets tested the perimeter up by Alaska, I recall, just to keep us on our toes. But they never seriously threatened us. Nevertheless, I was trained to stop them if needed without a second thought.

When I joined the astronaut program in 1966, the space race was still on. There were astronauts in Houston, such as Frank Borman, who made it very clear that NASA was not going to the moon for the glory of exploration. He devoutly believed we were doing it for one reason alone: to beat the Soviets. To him, this was a battle.

None of that was ever a big deal to me.

Going to the moon . . . now, that was a huge deal. I thought it would be wonderful if we could beat the Russians in the process, but I didn't think it all rested on that. The whole point to me was that we could put astronauts on the moon and bring them back. I don't remember many conversations about the Russians. I think most of our conversations were focused on the notion that "we need to do what we need to do." In retrospect, before we ever got anybody on the moon, the Russians were beginning to learn they couldn't. They had their big N1 launch vehicle, which was, in theory, even more powerful than our Saturn V rocket. They tried to launch it four times, and each time, it failed. So they gave it up and focused on Earth-orbit stuff instead.

There were folks in the States who had access to classified data, spy-satellite stuff, and knew about those giant Soviet rocket failures. I never did. In the Astronaut Office, we were aware, in a very general sense, that they had a huge rocket launch vehicle. It turns out that they had already designed a lunar lander. They had everything they needed, but they couldn't get the launch vehicle to successfully fly.

I wonder, if it had been widely known that the Russians were falling behind, whether we would have stretched out our program and been more relaxed about it. We didn't. We kept really pushing hard; we launched every few months, stayed on schedule, and did the job. By the time *Apollo 11* launched, it seemed clear the Russians were never going to make it. I think the pressure came more from within ourselves, to prove that we could do it.

After we landed on the moon, the Soviets told the world that they had never planned to go there at all. They said they'd always planned on building space stations instead. We got a big laugh out of that. I don't think anybody believed it for one minute. I think the Soviets had got to a point where they said, "You know, we're like anybody else—we've only got so much money to spend. We can't keep launching failures." By then, it was too late for them to regroup and do something different. That's when they gave up and said, "Well, we'll focus on Earth orbit."

Other information came from the Soviets a lot more freely. There was always a sort of information underground that came our way about what was going on. It was kind of a friend-to-friend sort of thing; I don't think there was ever anything official about it. For example, the Russians called us after they lost three guys on reentry during the *Soyuz 11* mission in 1971. They told us what went wrong and why the crew died. A valve had been jarred open when two parts of their spacecraft separated just before reentry. That caused us to redo some of our procedures. We wore pressure suits any time we were docking, undocking, or any other time there was a situation where we might lose cabin pressure.

The panoramic camera I operated around the moon to take high-resolution photos while I orbited was modified from a version used by the U-2 spy plane. Because of this Cold War history, we could only use it under one condition—we should never point it at the Soviet Union. What good would a photo of the Soviet Union be from 250,000 miles away? That dumb rule was always a mystery to me. I didn't care to point it at them anyway. Who cared? That was a nonsense thing.

Before we went to the moon, our commander, Dave Scott, contacted a famous sculptor in Belgium named Paul Van Hoeydonck. He and Dave worked a deal, because Dave, Jim Irwin, and I had talked about this a lot: Wouldn't it be nice if we could put something on the surface of the moon commemorating all the guys who had been lost in space or in pursuit of the space program? We wanted to include all the Russians. So Dave contacted Hoeydonck, and they worked out this little aluminum figure. Dave placed it on the surface of the moon, with a little plaque. There were fourteen names on it—six of them were cosmonauts. The Soviets were still pretty secretive about their program back then. Had we known about Valentin Bondarenko, the cosmonaut who died in 1961 in a training accident, we would have included him. If anyone ever goes back up to that landing site and our memorial, please add his name for us.

When we splashed down in the ocean at the end of the *Apollo 15* mission, apparently there was a Russian tug just a few miles away, shadowing our recovery forces. The press reported that when our parachute failed, they offered assistance. It was politely declined. So they were there, keeping an eye on us, seeing how we were doing. They were obviously there to pick up intelligence if they could, but I believe they were also there to see that we got down safely.

So personally, I've never had a problem with Russians. When I have met cosmonauts, we've always had a good time together. I think that was because we were a small, select group, all in the same business. Yeah, they were Russians, and we were Americans. But so what? We were all doing the same thing. We were cheering for each other. This was something that involved everybody. It was different from politics. It was the governments that had the problems with each other. That was where we ran into the Cold War issues— mutually assured destruction and that kind of thing. But people to people, we were the same type. Some of them are even friends with me on LinkedIn and Facebook now.

I think that happens a lot in life; we end up being closer to our enemies after a war is over than we are to our friends. I mean, we did incredible things for Germany after the war, and the same for Japan. I think that's why, although we've had our ups and downs, Japan's pretty loyal to this country. Germany is less so these days, because they've gotten so big and important and powerful— they don't need us anymore.

International friendship is the impetus behind the Association of Space

Explorers. There's only one entry requirement to be a member. You have to have orbited Earth at least once. It's a global forum to promote exploration, emphasizing international friendship. Over forty countries have officially flown someone in space now, and that's not even counting folks who were born overseas and can claim to be the first spacefarer born somewhere in particular. Since 1985 the association has been getting as many spacefarers as they can together somewhere in the world each year.

It is attended by everybody. Lots of people from the United States and Russia, who are then joined by all the other countries—England, France, Germany, Italy—whoever has put somebody into space. China hosted one in 2014. I was very pleased about that. I don't see why we've had a problem cooperating with the Chinese, simply because politically our governments do not quite agree. It seems like a silly thing, because there's this old axiom about keeping your friends close but your enemies closer. I guess maybe I hold different opinions than the common ones, but I think we ought to be working with the Chinese and not arguing with them. It seems to me that the more we get involved with them, the better off we'll be. At air shows in China, they have big space displays, with a bunch of their astronauts in attendance. Thousands of kids are there; they jam the place. They are really into it, just as we were in the 1960s. I often feel disappointed that we don't have that kind of attention here—crowds of people who really think space exploration is the right thing to do. I think a lot of that is because we don't hear about it much in this country anymore. The media has backed away, and the government rarely says anything about it. So it's just kind of a quiet dark horse that's sitting back there not doing anything. Events such as the Association of Space Explorers annual conference remind me of the enthusiasm that is out there in the world.

While I like the Russians, however, I'm not naive. While the Cold War was still on, I was well aware that things could turn hostile. For most of the last decade, we've also been in a position where the Russians are playing hardball with us. We jointly operate the International Space Station with them, but since we retired the space shuttle in 2011, they've had the only operating spacecraft capable of sending crews up and down. They're more than partners—they are driving the program. Because they're the only game in town, they put the price way up when flying NASA astronauts. I would be doing the same thing if I were them. It's what the market will bear. If the Russians take two of our people, NASA pays them over $170 million. They've probably paid for their whole launch right there. They've been very successful at it. The Russians have the most reliable launch vehicle in the world. They've been flying the same thing for sixty years now, and they incrementally improve it as they go. It just gets better and better. I suspect the day will come when they're going to have to do something different, but I don't see that on the horizon any time soon.

Have you ever seen inside one of their little Soyuz spacecraft? It is tiny. Anyone riding one of those is curled up with their knees to their chin. With three people in there, there is no room to move. I'd probably have some problems with that confinement. I think I could get a little claustrophobic. The Apollo command module was a pretty good size. We had room to maneuver, we had room to reach around and do things, and we were stretched out on couches. I guess the Russians train the people who launch with them so that they get pretty comfortable in there. But I'm thankful they at least give us a way to get to the space station and back. It's a far cry from the days I was on constant alert in a fighter squadron, ready to kill them.

When I was in orbit around the moon, I'd worked with our geology trainer, Farouk El-Baz, on translations so that I could read the phrase "Hello Earth; greetings from *Endeavour*" in nine foreign languages every time I came back into radio contact. Of course, I included Russian too. It may well be the only time anyone has spoken a Russian sentence in lunar orbit—for now. One day, the Russians will be speaking it there themselves. Until then, I hope they liked my effort to make them feel included.

4

The Twelve

The public perception of what astronauts did on a flight to the moon is different from the reality. The media tends to focus on those who walked on the moon. I've begun telling people when I give a talk that while only twelve guys walked on the moon, forming a very exclusive club, there's another club that's even more exclusive. It's the command module pilots who orbited the moon solo while the others landed. There are only six of us. It doesn't always go over well, and I don't expect it to. But I do it to make a point. "Oh, you walked on the moon," is considered the high point for any astronaut by the public. But I have to tell you that it depends on what you were doing on the mission. The lunar module pilot may have walked on the moon, but he was a passenger. He didn't do any flying; he looked at the instruments during the descent to the surface, just along for the ride. The commander did the few minutes of flying to and from the surface. The command module pilot—my job—flew everything else in the mission. We flew all the way out to the moon and all the way back, plus we stayed in lunar orbit while the others landed. It's not considered dramatic or newsworthy. However, I love to fly, so I considered it a great job. If you're into piloting, my job was the big deal. If you're into walking on the moon, which is more where the general public's mind is, then it doesn't matter who was flying. My job of command module pilot has become the forgotten one.

I can tell you what the other Apollo astronauts were like—who these individuals were. They were all very different, that's for sure. I'll begin by telling you about the twelve whom the public gravitate toward most—the moonwalkers. They experienced something that no other humans have, before or since. Can you imagine what it is like to walk somewhere that is not on this planet?

Apollo 11

Neil Armstrong

Neil was probably the greatest gentleman I've ever met. I didn't know him well when I was in the program, but I got to know him better after we were both out of NASA and I was running the Astronaut Scholarship Foundation. Neil was an absolute gentleman about everything.

I think the reason Neil felt friendly toward me is because I never bugged him. He had hundreds of requests for his time, all the time. But Neil absolutely focused on the things that were important to him, such as raising money for Purdue University. He was the chair of their fundraising committee for a couple of years and raised a lot of money for them. I wrote to Neil one day and said, "We really need you, and you could really help us, would you do something with the Foundation?" And he wrote back, very nicely, and said, "Al, I'd love to help you, but I spend my energies where I think they're going to do the most good. Right now, I'm raising money for Purdue. We are committed to raising a billion dollars. I have to put all of my effort into this, so I cannot do the Foundation too. I can't get spread too thin."

I wrote back and said, "I understand perfectly, don't worry about it, I will never ask you again." And I never did. I think that's one reason Neil and I were pretty good friends, because he appreciated that. I gave him an honest answer, and he was good. That's the kind of guy Neil was; if you asked him to do something that he was not willing to do, it was okay, because he'd tell you no. But if you kept bugging him, then he would really turn off. He did not appreciate people putting pressure on him.

In the years after I left NASA, I used to run into Neil at aviation conventions around the country. He was with a small company that made software for light airplanes. One time, Neil was clear on the other side of the hall, and when I walked in, he came all the way over to catch up with me. I believe it was because I wasn't pushing him for anything. I had no motive for talking to him other than to say, "Hi, Neil. I'm here. What's going on?"

If people annoyed him, he would just disappear. He never got nasty. Neil was the sort of individual who kept above the fray. He always played it a little bit more high level than a lot of the guys. If he was at a banquet and too many people came around, he would discreetly slip out. That's the way he handled it; he simply didn't want to be bothered.

Neil was a very important figure in aviation, but he was not out there promoting himself. The last thing he was interested in was being a famous person. Yet I would never call Neil a recluse. He was out a lot doing things—people just didn't know it. Neil channeled his efforts into projects that would be productive, which is very different from getting publicity. I think Neil was really good at doing stuff like that. He was very honest, open, sincere, and deeply conscious of his place in history.

Let's compare Neil to Yuri Gagarin, the first person in space. Gagarin was the most famous guy in the world when he flew in 1961. Even bigger than the Beatles, because there was only one of him. So he was it. I think it ruined him. The popularity, the adulation, and the fact that the Russian government paraded him everywhere—I felt so sorry for the guy. He tried his best, but he was a little pilot who happened to be the first guy they picked to fly in space. He knew that he really didn't have anything to do on the flight except to ride along, so the flight could've been made by anybody. But it was him, and he became a world hero. Initially, he was probably very aware of the fact that he just happened to be the first. But I think the more that kind of fame is imposed on someone, the more they begin to believe the media and the things that are said about them. They're a big star. I think he was a decent guy, from all I've heard. However, the attention lavished on him let him spread his wings a little bit more than he should have. I think the pressure of all the publicity and the public appearances pushed him into some bad behavior, because it was a tough thing to handle. He became notorious for drinking and chasing women. When thousands of women are pursuing you like crazy, most guys would probably do the same thing. He didn't even really have to chase anybody—they were there. That has to mess with a guy's mind. It's sad. He was a very simple, humble, nice guy who got thrust into the spotlight to a point where he had a hard time with it.

Neil was in the same boat—perhaps even more so. But he was smart, and he didn't let it get to him. Neil remained humble and made few public appearances. After his *Apollo 11* flight, he did what President Nixon wanted, but following that, you didn't hear much about him. He reverted to being a college professor and doing his thing. Perhaps if Yuri had been allowed the opportunity to do something like that, he might still be alive. I think Gagarin didn't have any choice. The Russian government really put pressure on him to do all those things. They didn't care what happened to him. They just wanted the publicity. And they got it. That kind of government pressure, media pressure, and social pressure—Neil didn't let that drive him. That was smart—as opposed to other people who not only recognize their place but also promote it, market it, and sell things because of it.

I think Neil did a lot of reading about aviation pioneer Charles Lindbergh and patterned the way he did things after him. The irony was, of course, the more Neil stayed out of the limelight, the more people were after him. I remember walking in on Buzz Aldrin's then-wife Lois complaining that Neil didn't go out and market himself. I asked her, "Why are you saying that?" She replied, "Because if he did, that would be more opportunities for Buzz."

I was not happy with that and told her so. "Lois, you are dead wrong. In the first place, it's none of your goddamn business what Neil does or doesn't do. Buzz has got to stand on his own. Leave Neil alone. He's a nice man, and he does not like to be pushed."

Public interest in Neil Armstrong was inversely proportional to the number of times he was out in the public. The more he played Lindbergh, the more the public wanted him. That's why I think he became such an icon in the space program. He did not swamp the market with himself, which would have diminished the image he projected to the world. Neil was always a little bit aloof, a little bit away from it, a little bit in the shadows. I do believe there was another strong purpose behind that—things he did come out about publicly were very important to him.

Forget making a lot of money. Neil was well off. He had a couple of directorships, and they paid him well. So money was not an issue, but doing worthwhile things was. He reserved himself for those things that were really meaningful—not just a little conference here, a conference there, or a weekend signing autographs. He never did that.

I still smile when I recollect one encounter with Neil. For the twenty-fifth anniversary of *Apollo 11*, there was a celebration in Washington DC. My wife, Jill, and I went up for that, and we were all staying at a residential-type hotel downtown. We were given a key to our room at check-in and told, "There's a hospitality suite if you want to go there, too, clear at the end of the hall on the twelfth floor."

So we went up there, and Neil's wife answered the door when we knocked.

"Oh!" I said. "We thought this was the hospitality suite."

"No, no, no, this is Neil's suite. This is where he stays."

"Okay, well, I'm really sorry. I didn't mean to bother you."

As we got ready to leave, I heard Neil yell out, "Hey! Is that you, Al?"

"Yeah, yeah, yeah, it's me."

"Come on in here; I want to talk to you."

Neil was stretched out on the sofa, with his shoes off, just relaxing. He was going over his notes for the talk that night. So I sat down, and we started chatting. After a few minutes, he handed me a sheaf of papers and said, "This is my speech tonight. Would you read it over and tell me what you think?"

I was pleased to be asked. So I read through it.

"Is there anything I'm missing or anything that maybe ought to be added?" he asked.

I thought the beginning was lacking something, so I shared some ideas with him on how to start. Jill and I went to the event that night and were seated in the front row with Neil right next to us. They introduced him; he got up, looked at me, and started laughing. Then he went up to the podium, and he did exactly what I had suggested he do. I must admit—that felt very special.

Around the fortieth anniversary of his moon mission, Neil did me a big favor. He meticulously read the manuscript for my memoir *Falling to Earth*, made a number of minor technical amendments, and gave us a great deal of glowing praise in emails such as this one: "It is a very good book, clearly and carefully written. When I am reading an aeronautic or space book I usually have questions on every page. I got all the way to page 103 before I questioned the description of the accelerometers on the inertial platform."

He went on to provide an extremely positive front-cover blurb for the book, mentioning how my role of command module pilot was greatly underappreciated by the public.

The fortieth anniversary of each Apollo mission was celebrated in a different city in the country. Space fans began to realize that Neil was discreetly showing up to each one and making a carefully crafted speech about that specific flight. Insiders knew he was appearing only if his name was not used in promotions of any kind. Some of those events were fundraisers, a type of event he usually never did, but he broke his own rule on this occasion to honor his fellow astronauts.

We reached the fortieth anniversary of the *Apollo 15* flight, and there was a celebration event at the Cape. Dave Scott and I were there, along with Jim Irwin's family and many other Apollo astronauts. As part of the evening,

Neil gave a speech in the Saturn V building. I expected him to talk about the entire *Apollo 15* mission. After all, Dave Scott was not only the *Apollo 15* commander, but he'd also flown in space with Neil on *Gemini 8*.

Neil's whole speech was about the underappreciated role of the command module pilot. It was like a greatly expanded version of the quote he had just provided for my book's front cover. I was dumbfounded. I mean, Dave was sitting right there, yet the speech was almost all about what I did. He clearly wanted to make a point that command module pilots were the backbone of a flight. I was blown away. I thought it was wonderful that he picked me out. I loved it.

Yet I didn't even have a chance to talk to him and thank him afterward. Everything got away from us, and I never got him alone. So wherever you are, Neil—thank you. That meant a lot.

After he passed away, I got involved in the making of a movie about him, named *First Man*. It was based on a book by my friend Jim Hansen, and I was a technical consultant. I helped them with some of the details on mission procedures and mostly was just there to answer questions. It was fascinating to watch them film the lunar surface re-creations.

The movie ended up being about Neil, his troubles, and his achievements. Ryan Gosling was superb and played it perfectly. The movie made Neil out to be more aloof than he really was, I believe, but that's just my opinion. I'd say he was more self-contained than aloof. While there were some parts about Gemini and Apollo, the movie was mostly about Neil and his family. It was not about space; it was about a man. I wasn't sure about the scenes where they showed a lot of shaking motion, and the background music was too loud. Nevertheless, I thought it was really good overall. I was certainly much happier with it than I had been with parts of the *Apollo 13* movie, which I think made Jack Swigert out to be less of an outstanding astronaut than he truly was. There's always movie nonsense like that. Just look at the charade they made of Gordon Cooper's character in the movie *The Right Stuff*. By comparison, *First Man* was wonderful.

I think, in the long run, people are probably going to remember Neil more than anybody else from the space program. He was my hero and a good friend. I miss him. When I see the stupid stuff that gets attention in the media, I appreciate how he dealt with fame more each day. I loved the guy. He was really nice.

Buzz Aldrin

To be honest, I think Buzz is a sad character. I know he has battled a lot of emotional and psychological problems over the decades. He had problems when he was in the program that I was witness to but won't recount. Then I think after *Apollo 11*, alcohol and clinical depression got to him.

When we were at NASA, he was never good socially. He could have been a standout; he came into the program with an impressive background. Although he'd never been a test pilot, he'd been a combat pilot during the Korean War. He earned a doctorate in orbital mechanics, making him one of the world's experts on how spacecraft could rendezvous and dock in orbit. Yet he was never really close to anyone in the Astronaut Office. He was not an outcast, but people were standoffish with him. Something felt a little off.

I remember when I was going through astronaut selection. I underwent about three days of psychological testing. I asked the psychiatrist, an air force colonel, "Can you keep anybody out of the program?"

He replied, "No. We can't."

"Well, why have psychological testing?"

"If we run across somebody who's clinically insane, then we can let the board know, and they'll probably drop him off the list. But short of that, we can't really do anything."

Buzz has been very honest—brave, in fact—in sharing his battles with depression. I wonder if he would have had a much happier life if those issues had been caught earlier—perhaps during his NASA application—and he'd received the treatment he eventually sought.

After leaving NASA and spending time in a hospital, Buzz was in pretty bad shape. When he was able to work again, he ended up in LA, selling cars in a showroom. As the decades went by, I was pleased to see him gain a level of stability in his personal and professional life.

Much as I would like that to be a happy ending, Buzz Aldrin's second act was the one I found the hardest to deal with. This falls into two parts.

First is Buzz's relentless advocacy, promoting his ideas to go to Mars and beyond. Some of them are mathematically elegant. But I have a hard time dealing with him, because I can't get him to talk about anything else. He's so hung up on his plans to get humans to Mars that it's gotten to the point where I personally believe it's an obsession. I think the relentlessness of it has now become a negative. After a while, people tire of seeing his charts and diagrams of complex orbits for solar system exploration. I know—because they told me—of at least two NASA administrators who told their staff that if Buzz called wanting a meeting to pitch his ideas, they were to tell him the administrators were out of town. Buzz haranguing people about going to Mars got old fast.

I ran into Buzz in a hotel in London some years ago, where we'd both been booked to do an autograph event. Buzz was in the middle of the lobby, talking to fellow astronaut Bruce McCandless and Ellen, Bruce's sweetheart of a wife. As I came close, I heard what he was talking about. He was trying to convince Bruce about how we should go to Mars and why we should do it. He was giving him the whole pitch.

I had to say, "You know, Buzz, you're talking to the wrong people! Bruce doesn't care about going to Mars. What are you doing?" But Buzz was so focused that he didn't hear anything I said. He started in again and wouldn't stop. Eventually, to get him off the subject, I asked him about his wife, and that finally broke the spell.

For the Saturday night dinner at one of those English events, they asked Buzz to be the keynote speaker. It was a general crowd of families relaxing for the evening, at what was primarily an autograph show, not even particularly space themed. Buzz got up and, for an hour, gave a complex lecture on the technical issues of going to the moon and Mars. He lost the whole room. I watched them all tune him out. He doesn't seem to understand that he doesn't connect with an audience at all. I certainly can't get through to him, and I've tried.

I feel bad for him, because he's spent the last few decades pushing his space plans, and he may well have inspired some people. But overall, I'm sad to say he probably turned thousands more off. All that effort, and in the end, his effect will probably be zero, or a negative number.

My other thought about Buzz is my intense dislike of what he has done with Apollo's legacy. He has used the *Apollo 11* mission and his part in walking on the moon to promote whatever he happens to be selling. I don't think he was good at any of that until he married his third wife, Lois. She had a talent for marketing. She pushed him and got him pretty successful again. He'd been at rock bottom in his life not long before, so in some ways, she was healthy for him. But as he did more and more shilling, he was violating all the unspoken rules and conditions we had lived under. He was promoting himself based on

Apollo 11 so that he could make money. I think he's the only one in the program who really did that. If you go to a conference where Buzz is, he usually has a table piled high with T-shirts of himself that he's selling.

It's probably not unethical, but it is certainly not a good thing to do in my opinion. I think there's no question that it cheapens the whole moon landing. I particularly didn't like the title he gave himself and plastered all over his souvenirs for sale: "Rocket Hero." I believe hero is a title bestowed on you by others. Not one you choose for yourself, as marketing.

If Buzz were to do it right, he would be revered. But instead, I believe he's become a joke. He shows up on TV in the wrestling ring. He shows up performing awkward rap tunes. That kind of thing bothers me. He has promoted himself so widely that his name is more important than who he is.

I particularly thought his celebrity turn on the *Dancing with the Stars* TV show was an embarrassment, not only for him but for what he represents. His appearance was a disaster. It made the space program look like a Disney attraction, while diminishing the status of astronauts. I think he made a fool of himself. My daughter really wanted me to apply for that show, too, but I said no. One disaster was enough.

Buzz has turned ninety. I think it's too late for him to change. I wish it wasn't.

Apollo 12

Pete Conrad

When Pete Conrad was asked about flying to the moon—which was often—his response might surprise you.

"You know, it's just another flight."

I don't think Pete actually felt that way. I knew him well enough to know that commanding a moon landing meant a bit more, but that was his response. Hey, we're test pilots. This is what we do. Just another flight. He was that cool and professional. I thought at the time—and I still think—the two best commanders in the program were Neil Armstrong and Pete Conrad. It's subjective and hard to quantify. It's just a feeling I have. We all thought Pete would be the first person to set foot on the moon.

I was the backup command module pilot for his *Apollo 12* mission, so it was my job to strap the crew in. I was inside the spacecraft before they got there, checking all the switch settings. The crew arrived, laughing and cracking jokes on the way. Once all the switches were set right, I got them in their couches, put their restraint harnesses on, and hooked up their oxygen and radios. Then I climbed out of the spacecraft, and the hatch was closed.

Back at the viewing stand, it was really raining hard. I never gave it a thought. I stood there in the rain and watched them lift off, when all of a sudden— KAPOW! A lightning strike, right on the spacecraft. Without missing a beat, Pete began reading off every instrument he could while he and the crew fixed the problems and kept right on into orbit. That had to be pretty goddamn scary. But Pete was doing what he was supposed to.

Pete was a unique individual. When he was around, I was never shut out. If you were on his team, man, you were on his team. He didn't need to announce he was in charge—he was just in charge. He was a short guy, but it made no difference at all. He could have been seven feet tall, and it would have been the same. His philosophy in life was, "You work really, really hard, and you have a lot of fun. But you work hard."

I envied that he was picked in NASA's second group of astronauts, because those guys got to fly a lot. By the time he commanded *Apollo 12*, it was already his third space mission. He was a great commander who took care of his crew. They were always together; they were like brothers. He was very good at what he did, organizing how his crew trained and flew in space. He worked Dick Gordon and Alan Bean really hard. They were an extremely competent crew, the tightest crew of any that flew. He and Dick and Alan were a unit. They also had a lot of fun.

Pete was my buddy. But then, Pete got along with everybody. He was a storehouse of stories, and all his stories were fun. He was always the center of attention. He'd sit and captivate people with his tales. He was a funny, funny guy and everybody's friend.

I got to know Pete pretty well, because we both raced sports cars together, back in Florida in 1969 and 1970. We were driving Formula Vees. Pete had a car, I had a car, and our friend Jim Rathmann's wife, Kay, had a car. We'd go up and down the coast, driving in all the races. Pete and I had a blast. He always thought he was a great driver, but he didn't have a whole lot of sense. He'd stick his foot on the accelerator and never take it off. Once, we were driving in the Paul Whiteman Classic at Daytona, and there was a chicane on the course. Pete raced toward it, hell bent for leather. Kay Rathmann was in her car, in front of him. Bang! He drove right into her, at full speed. He ran into his own teammate. He just never backed off. That was Pete. He never backed off anything.

There was always the question of what Pete should say when he stepped onto the lunar surface. Neil Armstrong's words, "That's one small step for man, one giant leap for mankind," were pretty famous by then. So the three of us on the backup crew were trying to figure out what we could suggest for a little guy like Pete. We shared some ideas with him and sprinkled a whole bunch of comments and suggestions throughout his checklists all the way to the moon.

He ended up using one of our suggestions: "Whoopie! Man, that may have been a small one for Neil, but that's a long one for me."

Pete always had a story or a joke to tell, and he was the center of attention wherever he went. I think of him with his bald head and gap in his teeth, and I picture him laughing. He was always laughing about something. Plus, Pete was loyal to his crew of Dick Gordon and Alan Bean for the rest of his life. And I think they always had the same loyalty to him. I miss him.

Alan Bean

Alan Bean was a great artist and a very good astronaut and pilot. I have put those three career achievements in that order because I think it describes him best. Twelve people landed on the moon, but only one of them captured what they saw in oils.

Alan really utilized his lunar flight to do something with his artistic talent. I found that pretty phenomenal. I remember looking at the moon myself when I orbited it, and it seemed mostly devoid of color. Alan took those hints of color he saw on the surface, combined them with imagination, and captured the dreamlike quality of the experience.

His paintings are wonderful. Alan was a really talented guy, both from the flying side and from the art side. That combination makes for a unique individual.

I think if you had asked Alan, he would have said his artwork was more important than going to the moon. What he did over decades of oil painting leaves a permanent exhibit of what went on during the moon missions. Sadly, *Apollo 12* is likely to get lost in history, as *Apollo 11* gets all the glory. Yet those paintings are going to be around forever.

Alan was always friendly and helpful when I was in the Astronaut Office. He was precise and thorough when he took on a task. He and I got along especially well in the last few decades of his life. We used to talk and text all the time. He was of immense help putting together the fortieth anniversary celebrations of the *Apollo 15* flight, including reading the riot act to some people who needed it. He was a wonderfully supportive friend when my book *Falling to Earth* came out. The quintessential nice guy who would go all the way to support projects and people he believed in; he was also one of the best when it came to interacting with the public. Alan would happily spend a long time with each person, answering their questions and finding out all about them in turn.

While he came across as a smiling, cuddly guy, believe me, he had a backbone of steel. Some people misread his amiable nature and thought Alan was a quiet little mouse sitting back in the corner. No way. When he needed to, he would tell people exactly what he thought. That was one of the many things I liked about Alan. There was no pretense. No bullshit. He'd just flat out say it.

Alan Bean was the perfect choice to land on the moon with Pete Conrad. The two of them each went on to command a mission on *Skylab*, America's first space station, and were perfect at that too. He passed away in 2018, and I can only think of all the paintings he wanted to do that we'll never see now.

Apollo 14
Alan Shepard

They called Al Shepard the Icy Commander, and that's true. He was not a friendly guy. A couple of years after becoming the first American in space, he developed a serious inner ear problem and was pulled from flight status for almost six years. While other astronauts flew Mercury, Gemini, and early Apollo missions, each vastly more sophisticated than his flight, he was grounded.

I'd watch Al Shepard come into the office for an hour or so in the morning. Then he'd leave and be gone for the rest of the day. That happened day after day. I found out later that he was in town with his friends and that they were developing big plans to build shopping centers and banks. So he really used his position as a springboard to get involved with very wealthy people. He parlayed his fame into something quite valuable. He was smart and also devious, feathering his own nest while he was the chief of the Astronaut Office. He worked his way into being a millionaire on government time, which was against the rules. I don't think anyone ever questioned Al Shepard about his outside business interests. Nobody seemed to care. I think he was immune at that point, since he was the first American in space.

I don't know what Al did even in the hour he was at work. He was not a boss. Deke Slayton was the one who made all the flight assignments and who really decided who was going to do what and where. At the time, I was busy working my way through the system and getting assigned to a flight. All I saw was a guy who was not friendly. I saw Shepard at a distance, as the older, important guy who'd sit in a corner office, and I avoided him. I didn't want to get involved with any of that. Whatever I did in the space program, I wanted it to be based on my capability, not on office politics. I thought he didn't like me. But he probably didn't like anybody—that's simply the way he was. Al acted in an aristocratic way, as if he was above everyone he talked to. I suspect he really only had a good relationship with Deke Slayton. He and Wally Schirra didn't get along well. He and John Glenn didn't get along either.

Shepard eventually got his ear temporarily fixed. He was back on flight status. Then we witnessed a conjunction of this and another issue going on in the Astronaut Office. Gordon Cooper, another of the original seven astronauts, had basically cut himself out of the program. I did a lot of stuff with Gordo; he was a good friend. Yet I knew he was lackadaisical about some things. He was the *Apollo 10* backup commander, and if his work on that mission had gone well, he would have commanded *Apollo 13*. But he was racing cars at Daytona when he should have been working at the Cape to get ready for *Apollo 10*. Gordo was showing that he didn't care, at which point I think Deke Slayton said, "Okay. You're out. If you can't dedicate yourself to doing what needs to be done at the Cape, we don't need you in the program." You couldn't be lackadaisical about Apollo. Even Gemini was a pretty complicated spacecraft. Apollo was a different order of magnitude.

Al Shepard hadn't flown since 1961, and that flight had lasted fifteen minutes. He'd been forced to sit out the entire space race, right up to the moon landing. He never had the background training and experience everybody else had. But he wanted a flight. Al Shepard was too big a name for anybody to disagree with. He was simply too important, too powerful. And he was ready to give up his job as chief of the Astronaut Office to make the flight. So Deke put him straight onto *Apollo 13*. The problem then was that Al needed more time to train. So they switched the crews of *Apollo 13* and *14*. This gave him enough time to train for it—assuming he took it seriously. Plus, he had the talented Ed Mitchell and Stu Roosa on his crew, which was a huge help to him.

When *Apollo 13* didn't land on the moon, *Apollo 14* was tasked with touching down at the same planned location. The cost of two Apollo missions—a huge expense—was now being invested in learning the geological secrets of a single landing site. The delay while NASA fixed the issues from *Apollo 13* gave Al even more time to train. There was only one problem—Shepard made it clear he did not care about geology.

Ed Mitchell, his lunar module pilot, was the expert Shepard needed alongside him when landing. Stu Roosa, the command module pilot, could get them all to the moon and back. It really only left the lunar surface activities for Shepard to master. But he wasted the opportunity. Tired and overheated while making a sprint to a crater rim he and Ed Mitchell never reached, Shepard neglected to carefully document the rock and soil samples he gathered. They were still useful to scientists back home but nowhere near as much as if he'd trained well and done his job correctly.

What did Al care about? He took a couple of golf balls with him to the moon, because he had a major deal lined up when he came home to promote a golf company. When the Senate investigated this, he denied everything.

So when I was at NASA, I didn't think highly of him. To me, Al Shepard was not a leader. Al Shepard was only out for himself. Al Shepard looked after Al Shepard. That was it.

We became much friendlier when we were both out of the program. In the late 1970s and early 1980s, I began hosting Boy's Club fundraisers in the Palm Beach area. We'd have a big golf tournament, followed by a black-tie dinner. I'd never had a good relationship with Al before, but I'd call him out of the blue and ask, "How about coming down?"

"Oh sure!" he'd reply. "When is it?"

I never had to ask him more than once. He came in his own corporate airplane. After attending a number of these events, he saw how successful it was to get former astronauts together to raise money for good causes.

In 1984 I learned he was creating the Mercury Seven Foundation, along with the other surviving original Mercury astronauts. Their aim was to provide scholarships for students. The idea was not simply to get kids in college but to fund those who could really make a difference in the future. They were trying to provide scholarships for the best and the brightest. I really wanted to be a part of that, so I wrote to Al, saying, "I am only an hour away, I can really help, why not put me on the board?" By and by, he did. I don't know if Al Shepard ever really thought much of me, but I lived close by, so I could be helpful.

I spent time on the board. I just hung with it. When Al eventually left, Jim Lovell took over—and frankly, I felt more comfortable.

Al Shepard passed away in the summer of 1998. By 2005, feeling I could really do some good for the direction of the foundation, I ran for the position of chair and was given the job. By then, it had been renamed the Astronaut Scholarship Foundation.

The work I did there was some of the most rewarding and fulfilling of my life. We raised millions of dollars for students who are out there today doing amazing work. They've already helped create a better future.

So, Al, while I was never really a fan of yours, I'm really glad you started that foundation. It gave me the chance to do some really meaningful and positive work.

Ed Mitchell

Ed was known as the smartest guy in my astronaut group.

I knew Ed before NASA. When I was at test pilot school at Edwards, Ed was there as well. He was a good pilot, but he was a brain too. Ed Mitchell knew all the engineering stuff. He was a considered, thoughtful, and well-rounded guy. He graduated first in his class, which surprised no one.

When we both were selected by NASA, the agency assigned us six months of training classes. As I mentioned earlier, after about a week, I got together with Ed and Charlie Duke. We agreed we could teach the courses better—and so we did. That's how smart Ed was; he could easily replace his own teachers.

Ed was soon tasked with detailed work on building and testing the lunar module at the manufacturer in Long Island. I was doing the same, except with the command module in Downey, California. Our paths didn't cross much, but together we did a lot to refine both Apollo spacecraft. We were both on the support crew for *Apollo 9*, doing all we could to make the mission a success.

Ed was named to the backup crew for *Apollo 10*, along with Gordo Cooper and Donn Eisele, but it soon became clear those three would never fly in space together. For different reasons, Gordo and Donn had little chance of sticking around. When Alan Shepard then took the flight from Gordo, he had his pick of astronauts. He kept Ed Mitchell on the crew, the only survivor from the *Apollo 10* backup slot. It was a wise choice for a number of reasons.

For one, Ed never got into any of the controversies that sometimes swirled around the Astronaut Office. He just did his job, and so there was no reason to remove him from the crew. He was solid. I think when Al Shepard was assigned to the flight, he took a look at Ed and said, "Hmm. He's a very smart guy; he'll be good for me to have." It was a natural choice.

I believe Shepard also wanted to fly with two people with less experience than him, to satisfy his own ego, which left only rookie astronauts. So he was paired with the two best unassigned guys in the office at the time—Ed and Stu Roosa. I think Ed learned much more than usual about the lunar module by being with Gordo Cooper, who never did anything. Ed had to learn it all to keep the crew safe, so he was extremely well prepared. Stu and Ed almost didn't need Al, except for the lunar landing, which Al flew. Although, I'm sure that Ed's steady stream of conversation, readings, and guidance greatly increased Al's chances of success.

I invited Ed Mitchell to move in with me when he and his wife Louise were separating. He ended up living with me for a long time. Ed did not start divorce proceedings at the time, because he was worried it might affect his astronaut career. He would not officially leave Louise until after his *Apollo 14* flight. He was afraid they would take him off the mission. I had a different take on all of that and had begun my own divorce, while at the same time hoping it would not cause my release from the program.

Ed was beginning to get interested in psychic phenomena, and he and I had many long, late-night discussions about it. He was getting into subjects most people couldn't understand, while also training to fly to the moon. He was smart enough to do it all.

In fact, I often thought Ed was too smart. In the Apollo program, he was great. But the psychic stuff became a bit of a joke to me. He was dead serious about it, though. He ended up trying an ESP experiment during the *Apollo 14* mission. His experiment, kept secret from NASA and done in his free time, was to pick a card out of a deck, hold it for a few minutes, and have four people back on Earth try to visualize the symbol on it. The results were poor, yet he decided this was proof that the experiment was a success. There was a statistical chance of picking the right card based on random numbers, and if there was some psychic connection, he hoped the number would be higher than the statistical average. In Ed's case, the number of right answers was so low he concluded there was, in fact, a reverse connection of some kind. I never did understand this conclusion, but Ed believed that it showed there was more happening than the laws of chance. He later built on this experiment to found the Institute of Noetic Sciences in California. I believe it is still there, doing research.

Because Ed was trying to keep all this quiet and out of the media, there was not a lot of talk about his experiments. He was now seen by his peers as a kind of offbeat mad scientist type, despite being a very competent lunar module pilot. Everyone mostly laughed at him about his ESP. His take on life is still suspect to most of the other astronauts from that time.

Being such a deep thinker, Ed pondered a lot more than those cards on the way to and from the moon. Seeing Earth from a distance made him consider the nature of existence. He said his consciousness was profoundly altered, and he gained a new perspective on civilization. Many of his ideas are elegant and beautiful.

You get a whole different perspective on life when you fly to the moon. I know I did. A lot of the ideas you have don't change dramatically, but over time, you begin to think differently. I think no matter what each one of us did after our missions, we were all affected, one way or another, by having made the flight. Everybody gained a slightly different perspective. You'll hear all the lunar astronauts talk about the view of a finite Earth in the blackness of space. It's a theme we all use, but I think it goes deeper than that. There were more things we were aware of after the flight than before. Yet it can stray too far. I thought Ed was a little off-the-wall—a little too carried away with his philosophies. He was also trying to do some funny things in his personal life, and to me it all seemed tied together.

In the early 1970s we were living close to each other again. I was working at NASA's Ames Research Center, while he was in neighboring Palo Alto, setting up his Institute of Noetic Sciences. He also remarried, to a woman named Anita, and they asked me to be the best man at their wedding. I didn't think they'd do well together, but I did it anyway.

They moved to Palm Beach, in Florida. Not long after, so did I, and once again we all reconnected. We continued to have a good relationship—until I ran for Congress in 1982.

Anita's profession was advertising and marketing. My opponent in the primary, Tom Lewis, hired her to do his campaign marketing. She pulled Ed into that. I'm not sure what Ed felt about the campaign one way or another, but I think he wanted to support his wife. So he went out publicly promoting my opponent, who ended up winning. There were a lot of nasty things done in the campaign by Lewis, some of which violated federal election laws.

I understand that politics is not about loyalty. But Ed turned out to be a very disloyal friend, after all the help I had given him. I'd given him a place to live when he and his wife split up, and I always felt he owed me more than a stab in the back. That was a big blow to me.

I was never as close to Ed after that. It ended our deep personal friendship. Looking back on it now, I think it was a bad thing for him to do, but I don't really hold it against him anymore. It was just a great shame it curtailed what had been a closer friendship. How could I deal with a guy who was publicly trying to get my opponent elected? I mean, that just doesn't work.

At a certain point, however, it was time to put it aside. It was sad to watch Ed deteriorate over the last few years of his life. He was still thoughtful and friendly and a nice guy to talk to. But he lost his teeth, was overweight, and couldn't walk far. It was clear something was badly wrong. In early 2016, forty-five years after he was preparing to fly to the moon, Ed died.

We lost the smartest and one of the humblest of the moonwalkers.

Apollo 15
Dave Scott

Professionally, Dave was the best there was. He was a star academic at West Point when I was there, in the very top percentage of his class. I became a battalion commander, but Dave was one step above, very close to being the First Captain. The guy was absolutely outstanding. I knew who he was when I was a teenager, and I ended up flying to the moon with him, which is weird to think about.

He's almost exactly the same age as me—we're only a few months apart. We both went to the University of Michigan and into the air force. He was selected for test pilot school, and I believe he got high grades there also. Dave was consistently outstanding and always exceptional in everything he did. He was a really bright guy—very dedicated, very detail oriented—and did all the things you'd think that kind of guy would do.

When NASA picked him, he became highly thought of there as well. He was the Boy Scout of the astronaut corps. In fact, they used to say, "You know what? He's going to be the chief of staff of the air force someday." We all thought he was such an icon for what an astronaut ought to be—a nice-looking guy who was very friendly, good with people, yet determined in what he did and tightly focused on what had to be done. I can remember going to meetings with Dave where he took copious notes. Then he'd take those notes, sort them into action items, and go down the list, taking care of each one. He knew everything that was going on.

He flew with Neil Armstrong for his first mission, *Gemini 8*. A thruster stuck on their spacecraft, which was a dangerous malfunction. It wasn't anything they did wrong; it was a malfunction in the machine. They were spinning once per second, and their vision was blurring. It could have resulted in them perishing—no question about it. Yet they persevered, quickly figuring out what was going on and taking the only corrective action they could. To survive before blacking out, they had to turn off one set of thrusters, turn on another set, and then fire the correct ones to reduce the rotation down to zero. Neil and Dave were fantastic test pilots to regain control and get home. The fact that they worked it out at all was a miracle. If I were spinning at one complete revolution per second, I would be really messed up. I don't know if I could have done what they did. But they did it. They survived.

What more can you say about two guys who can do that? They were the kind of coolheaded professionals we wanted in the program, because they could solve problems and do the right thing. I am sure many people looked at that incident and thought, "These guys are pretty superb. How the hell did they get themselves out of that situation?" It's probably a major reason why Neil was given command of *Apollo 11*.

Following *Gemini 8*, Dave flew again as the command module pilot on *Apollo 9*. That mission extensively tested the Apollo rendezvous and docking procedures. It was a really good crew, and Dave was once again a very competent pilot.

When given command of *Apollo 15*, Dave had to add another skill. He wasn't just a pilot anymore—he was now an explorer. Missions before *Apollo 15* had spent much less time on the surface. Plus, Al Shepard had annoyed many scientists by not taking his training seriously for the prior mission. Dave was different. He really wanted to know. He had geology professor Lee Silver work with him day after day. I think Dave not only knew what he had to do for our flight; he also really liked learning it. He could really have become a great geologist independently of NASA. He spent night and day studying; there was very little about the geology Dave did not understand. He was really dedicated to doing all the exploring he could. He wanted to take every minute, every second, to look at everything. He planned to take pictures, take panoramic shots, and drive the lunar rover to places he couldn't get to on foot. He looked forward to journeying to a deep rille on the moon and looking down into it. I can't tell you how delighted I was to be assigned to his crew.

We packed our flight plan with a lot more science than any other mission. We had more tasks than *Apollo 16* or *17* after us too. We included all the stuff the principal investigators wanted us to look at, even though the initial flight plan didn't include those things. Our attitude was, if we couldn't do it while we were in flight, we could always cross it off. But if we could find the time to do it, we would. In the end, we did it all. That's why *Apollo 15* is widely considered the most scientific flight.

When it came to planning all that with Dave, he pretty much went along with what I wanted to do. He was focused on landing and doing the surface stuff, but he also had to know some of the science we were doing in lunar orbit, because he and Jim Irwin would be there for a couple of days with me. We were in lunar orbit for six days, and they were only on the moon's surface for three. So Dave and I did a lot of stuff together, such as visual observations and taking photographs. I still always ran the scientific instruments in the SIM (scientific instrument module) bay and punched out the subsatellite we launched. But we worked well together on the parts we both did. There was an element of healthy competition between us, which made us do even more than we would have otherwise.

If you want a picture in your mind of what a real explorer looks like, to me, Dave Scott would be it. Just like polar explorers Scott and Amundsen—that's the persona Dave had. He was not a swashbuckling, take-on-any-odds kind of guy; he was a programmed, disciplined explorer. If you were to go on an Arctic exploration with a Dave Scott type, you would be very well prepared before you left. There would be no uncertainties about it. You would know what you were going to do. That was Dave, and that's why he was so good.

Of all the commanders, while John Young and Gene Cernan also did great scientific work on the surface, the two you hear about the most are Dave Scott and Neil Armstrong. Neil trained hard and had a great observational eye, finding a perfect variety of well-documented samples in a small area in a short amount of time. But he only had about two and a half hours out there on the surface. Dave had three days on the moon, plus a lunar rover to drive long distances. I think, in the long run, people are going to remember Neil more than anybody. But I would put Dave in that category too; professionally, Dave was right up there with Neil.

Dave and Jim did a phenomenal job of lunar exploration. Dave was so goal oriented; my God, he was going to do everything. He returned from the moon with his fingernails turning black, because he'd tightened up his space suit's gloves to the point where he was pushing the ends of the gloves all the time. He wanted to have that tactile feel when he was handling something.

Unfortunately, there can be a big difference between professional persona and individual character. Dave was the son of an air force general and had very high ambitions. Somewhere along the way, it seems he got off track. If we happen to be at the same function now, we avoid each other completely, although I am always very nice to Mag, his wife, whom I like a lot. If you've read my other book, where I discuss in careful detail what happened with those postal covers I mentioned earlier, you'll understand why that's the way it is between Dave and me. It's too long and detailed of a story to repeat. I trusted him with my life. There are things I have never heard him take responsibility for. I cannot, and should not, forgive the damage done to me, especially when it is clear I'll never receive an apology. I live with it and have formed my life so that I don't think about him much.

What he did outside of our flight to hurt me had nothing to do with the incredible success of our *Apollo 15* journey to the moon, which is what I have chosen to focus on here. These days, I'd much rather focus on the marvelous mission we flew together. Dave was the ultimate, perfect commander on the flight itself, heading the best trained, most ready, most scientific of any of the crews. I am proud to have been a part of that.

Jim Irwin

Jim never said an awful lot.

He was my officemate at NASA for a long time, and I got to know him well. When he and I were assigned to Dave Scott's Apollo crew, the mission planning discussions were usually between Dave and me, because we both had strong ideas. Jim was quieter, almost introverted, and generally went along with Dave's thoughts. He was a little closed off and never really confided anything, as if he didn't have thoughts of his own. He never argued.

The quietness, however, was deceptive. He was totally focused on his work, wordlessly went about his business, and ended up doing much more than was expected of him. Jim would work endlessly on something. He didn't work at a short-distance runner's speed; he worked at more of a marathon runner's pace. But he got there. He was a very thorough and detail-oriented guy, which I knew would be great for our crew.

I did not meet Jim until we were in the selection process for the program. Just like Dave and me, he was in the air force and had attended the University of Michigan. But we'd never met in college, as he attended classes many years ahead of me. He'd been at the same graduate school, taking a guided missile course that included aerodynamics, astronautics, and instrumentation, all designed to prepare us for guided missile projects. It was at a time when the air force was heavily involved with strategic missiles in response to the Cold War with the Soviets. Most of the students went into guided missiles, but a few of us went back to flying. Like Dave and me, Jim also went to test pilot school.

In 1961 Jim was flying with a student pilot who crashed the airplane. Jim was left with amnesia, his legs were in casts for over three months, and he was confined to a hospital bed. His jaw was wired shut, he had to eat everything through a straw, and he was told his right foot might have to be amputated. It's a sign of his quiet determination that he kept his foot; exercised his way back into regaining his flight status; and five years after the accident, was selected as an astronaut in the same group as me.

When I met him, Jim was buffed up. He exercised all the time. He was a runner and a weight lifter and looked terrific. He was a very handsome guy, and I thought he should have been on the beach at Santa Monica, showing off his muscles. It was hard to believe he'd been in such a bad accident. I think he was really conscious of that, so he kept in great shape.

Jim was the LMP (lunar module pilot) on our *Apollo 15* mission, but once he was on the lunar surface, he was absolutely at the same level as Dave, as a coexplorer. The difference between the commander and his LMP melted away.

Jim was extremely observant. He proved his worth and more when he and Dave spotted and carefully documented what came to be known as the Genesis Rock. It was an anorthosite, and geologists hoped it was a piece of the moon's primordial crust. It turned out to be about four billion years old. This was a major moment on our mission, and the geologists made a big issue out of it. That rock really told us a lot about the formation of the moon.

Both Dave and Jim got dehydrated on the lunar surface while pushing exploration to the limits. Jim lost too much potassium as a result and probably strained his heart. His heart rate was erratic when he came back up to rejoin me in lunar orbit, and he went into near arrhythmia. We were not told this at the time, only that we had to put him in a spacecraft couch and let him rest. One thing I've never understood—with Jim in the condition he was in, why did they give us the okay for me to do a space walk on the way back to Earth? I suspect that he had ingested enough liquid by then to get his potassium level back up to where his heart rate was okay. I was appalled when I found out later that they'd allowed him to get back in his pressure suit and float in the open hatch with a weakened heart. I guess mission control made a judgment call. They decided to take the risk that Jim would be okay—and he was. It turned out to be a much more serious problem, a life-threatening one, after he got back.

When the whole issue of the postal covers came up after our flight, Jim decided he was simply going to retire. I think he was ready to do that anyway. After such an embarrassment, both Jim and I knew there would be no more flights for us. Jim had the advantage of having more years in the air force by then, so he could retire with a full pension. I needed to stay in for a few more years, so I did.

After leaving NASA, Jim initially remained introspective. He even apologized to everyone for the cover incident. He had made a determination that he had been forgiven for it all by a greater power. I told him, "Jim, I don't know what this is all about, but your part in the cover thing is not something you ever needed to get anybody's forgiveness for."

I don't remember Jim getting into the religious thing much on our overseas tours after *Apollo 15*. Basically, we stuck to talking about the flight. After we got back from the tour, Jim started getting into the evangelical side of things.

I am not sure if the cover incident really affected Jim. I know how it affected me, but I was never quite sure how much of a downer it was for him. I think his retirement was the confluence of a bunch of events. His wife, Mary, who is very religious, wanted him to get more involved in the church, and Jim viewed giving Christian testimony, in part, as a way of gaining forgiveness. He and Mary formed the High Flight Foundation, and he began touring the world, spreading a religious message. Jim was a sweet, nice guy, the kind of guy who'd say, "You know, I did something wrong, but the Lord has forgiven me. I'm clean. I'm okay. I've been forgiven." I thought being the figurehead of such a public organization was a weird choice for him, because he was so easygoing and soft-spoken. I didn't think he was that kind of a leader at all. Yet he made a great success of it. So much so that he was away from home for almost the entire first year, giving speeches.

He overlooked the fact he was gaining weight and getting out of shape during this tour. He had his first heart attack soon after he came back. Jim had already committed himself to many more appearances. He called me to see if I could take care of some of them for him. I said yes, although I couldn't do them the way he did them. He was into religious testimony and talking about feeling the presence of God on the moon. I told him I couldn't do that. I wouldn't do it from a religious standpoint at all. I don't believe in it. I kept it on a religious-fellowship kind of level and told the audiences about my hopes for the world getting along despite cultural and political differences. I later went with Jim on one of his trips to Europe to help him out there too. We went to the Isle of Man and then from Glasgow to London, giving talks on the way. He asked me to be on his board also, and I accepted.

Jim and I were very close. We used to have long, friendly debates about some of the comments he made. He said he had started High Flight because when he was on the moon, he felt the presence of God. "Jim, you're full of shit," I used to say. "Come on, don't give me that crap. How could God be closer to you on the moon than he is here? How do you know he wasn't farther away? How do you know what direction God is coming from? You might be closer to him here on Earth than you were on the moon. That's nonsense!" But I think he was into the role he'd carved out for himself. It certainly worked from the viewpoint of public perception. People feel that the moon is an otherworldly body. Maybe Jim did too at that point.

Despite his heart attack, Jim continued his work with High Flight as if nothing had happened. He became a fanatic about running, focusing on it as the only thing to do, not the other health things he should have been trying. Running is great, but you've also got to have a good diet and peace of mind. I think Jim was under great stress all the time. I think of him as one of those quiet people who have some inner thing going on that doesn't show. I believe there was a lot of turmoil in him. He continued to tour and to run way too hard. He dropped a lot of weight, but he would not slow down.

The doctors discovered that Jim needed bypass surgery, which he survived. I don't know what goes through somebody's mind when they have a major issue like that, but I felt that Jim continued to ignore the warning signs. He kept doing the same kinds of things. Soon after, he had another close call. He was out jogging one morning in Colorado Springs—at the time, he lived about two blocks away from my brother Jerry—had another heart attack, and fell off the side of the road. A young kid happened to be going by at the time, saw him, and called 9-1-1. They were able to save him.

The last time I saw him, he'd lost even more weight and was still running many miles every day. In August 1991 he was up in the mountains on his mountain bike, with his cardiovascular surgeon, and had a last heart attack. The doctor put Jim in his s u v, raced him down to his house, put Jim in his spare bedroom, and tried to assist him, but there was nothing that could be done.

I went to Jim's funeral service at a big church in Colorado Springs. All the popular televangelists were there giving orations about him. It was flowery, Holy Roller stuff and a great service. Dave Scott was there, too, and later eulogized him as "the very best" when Jim was laid to rest at Arlington.

I always liked Jim. He was a really, really good soul. He was the first of the twelve moonwalkers to die. The chapter will close when the last guy goes. That'll be the end of it. Then it'll be pure history.

Apollo 16

John Young

In my mind, John Young was the consummate test pilot. He always said it exactly like it was. He never embellished and never tried to make anything any different than the truth.

Every spaceflight was a test flight, particularly during the Gemini program. On his second mission, *Gemini 10*, John was performing an untried type of rendezvous and was slightly off-line during his maneuvers. He overtook his target and then had to do a loop around to slow down and come back behind it. He told everybody, "I just made a mistake. We'll have to rework the procedures to make sure we do it right. But this is what happened, and this is what I did to recover from it."

If the indications were that he had actually made a mistake, John was very clear to say so. He did not pull any punches about anything. Whether it was him, the machine, the plans, or the objectives, John was always clear, honest, and right on top of it.

The problem with the space program is that everybody expects perfection. If something unplanned happened on a flight, there was always a feeling of, "Well, what did you do wrong?" Someone in management with an ego would often remark, "Oh, no, that's not the way it was. You made a mistake." They wouldn't accept that the procedures may not have been clear or that the machine didn't do what it was supposed to do. Who cares? Find out what went wrong, and fix it!

That's exactly why we flew those missions, to find these kinds of issues—that's why they're called test flights. John Young was the perfect guy to do that—a good commander and a great, great pilot. John was a really thoughtful guy. I believe that's why NASA kept him on for so long; they valued his opinion. For many decades, he held the record for number of spaceflights: two Gemini flights, two Apollo missions to the moon, and then two space shuttle flights. He was the ultimate spaceman. Jointly, the fifth American to orbit Earth and the first to orbit the moon solo, he finally retired as an active astronaut after forty-two years—a record that is unlikely to ever be broken.

His *Apollo 16* lunar landing mission came right after mine. He and Charlie Duke took their geology training as seriously as Dave Scott and Jim Irwin had for *Apollo 15*, and they quickly disproved an established theory about the formation of the lunar site they landed in.

John was a good, solid guy, really funny, with a very dry sense of humor. I think he approached everything from the same standpoint: "Here's what I've got to do on this flight. I need to look for these things, and if anything doesn't work out the way I think it's going to work out, then I've got to tell somebody about it. I've got to make sure people understand that this is something that needs to be changed." That's what a really good test pilot does when he flies a new airplane. He trained really hard before each flight, to be on top of every detail.

John was always extremely safety conscious. During the shuttle program, he became kind of an overseer of crew safety. He was planning on making his seventh spaceflight, to deploy the Hubble Space Telescope, when the *Challenger* accident occurred. John was rightfully critical of NASA management for allowing a chain of events to take place that killed a crew. But it meant that he was sidelined into a different job, and he never flew again.

Think about that for a second. NASA managers not only allowed a crew to die; they then sidelined someone who wanted to take a clear-eyed look at why it had happened. It gives you an idea of how bad NASA management could be. Honesty was not rewarded; it was punished.

John died in early 2018. In the space of just over a year, we lost six of America's most legendary astronauts and some of my closest friends. Gene Cernan, Paul Weitz, Dick Gordon, Bruce McCandless, John Young, and Alan Bean, all went one after another. That was pretty heavy.

John was probably the most honest guy in the program. He did not give a shit about protocol. If there was a problem, even if it was his fault, he let everyone know. He had a true test pilot attitude. He will be missed.

Charlie Duke

Charlie and I were in the same class in test pilot school, and we were selected by NASA at the same time. So I have known him for decades, and he has always been the same. He's a really friendly guy, with a twinkly eyed smile and that little southern drawl people really like. Millions of people around the world heard it when he served as CAPCOM in mission control for the *Apollo 11* moon landing, relaying information to Neil to help him land. Neil had chosen him specifically for this moment because of his familiarity with the lunar module's systems. It was a skill that proved very useful a few years later, when Charlie landed on the moon himself during *Apollo 16*.

He was a popular guy in the program, and he's a good man. When he left NASA, he followed a religious path, a little like Jim Irwin. He's out on the road a lot and gives a good talk, whether it's about religion or the moon. Being a more outgoing guy than Jim was, Charlie's talk has a lot more expressiveness and showmanship to it. He does a lot of good, traveling the world talking about the Apollo program with passion and enthusiasm.

I like Charlie. When after many years I resigned as the chair of the Astronaut Scholarship Foundation, Charlie took over and helped the important work continue. If the Apollo program had kept going and I had stayed at NASA, I would probably have been in line to command *Apollo 21*. The program would have ended with *Apollo 20* if the original schedule had held. But for discussion, let's say it happened. I would have wanted to take my friend Paul Weitz, but since this presumably would be the last moon landing, I would have picked a crew with experience. I would have asked Ken Mattingly and Charlie Duke to go along with me, with Ken as command module pilot—although Ken and I would have both wanted the command slot.

Charlie's a friend, and we always have a good time when we get together.

Apollo 17

Gene Cernan

The first and last moon landing commanders couldn't have been more different, personalitywise.

Neil Armstrong was quiet, humble, and thoughtful. Gene was a much more outgoing, oratorical type. He is going to be remembered for a long time, because he was excellent with the media and there are a lot of recordings of him out there. His speeches and quotes have made a big mark on the popular imagination.

Gene and I were friends. But it's hard for me to get a warm feeling about him, because he was everybody's Mister Spaceman. He'd come and do charity stuff for me and help out. I appreciated how he approached this, and he was very friendly when he saw me. But five minutes later he was gone. So he was a different sort of person, the kind who made everyone feel special for thirty seconds. I always thought Gene was almost too much of an icon of the space program.

His speeches were flowery; sometimes I found them a little overpowering. His talks were emotional, all-American, God bless the country, hearts and flowers stuff. I recognize, however, that I was not the target audience. He was trying to get the public to appreciate the meaning of the Apollo program, and he made it more about the experience than about himself. He could move a room like a master politician. While it was not really my thing, I must say he was really good at it.

There was never any guarantee Gene would command a moon landing. With only one mission left in the program, everyone wanted to be on that flight. It looked like Dick Gordon would get it, as he had Jack Schmitt on his crew. As the only geologist assigned to a crew, NASA had received overwhelming pressure to fly Jack. The only question was who would land with him.

Ironically, I think Gene having a flying accident sealed the deal in his favor. He crashed a helicopter into a river, and he fully admitted that it was his own fault. He never made any bones about it, never tried to fudge it. He just said, "Hey, this is what happened." He was upfront about it, and I think that helped him stay on course and get the flight. There were other people who were very bitter about Gene Cernan getting the flight. But I admired his honesty.

Apollo 15, 16, and *17* were the real human exploration highlights of NASA—

and in a way, for all humankind, before or since. Gene not only commanded an outstanding mission of exploration; he also knew how to relate it to the public.

I liked Gene—he was a good guy. If you know anyone who is cynical about space exploration, sit them in front of a recording of a Gene speech. They'll probably be in tears by the end of it and a lifelong convert.

Jack Schmitt

Jack Schmitt is one of the smartest guys I've ever known—and he will probably tell you that. If you go to a conference where Jack is in attendance, he will dominate the discussion, as he is a really brilliant academic. He worked very hard with our crew to get the lunar surface work just right. I think it was a good idea to send him on *Apollo 17*. He was definitely the brain of that crew and could do so much on the lunar surface.

NASA selected Jack in a group of scientist-astronauts in 1965. He was the only geologist. The scientists were chosen for their scientific expertise and did not have to have any piloting experience. You can imagine how this was viewed by folks such as Alan Shepard, who cared little for science. The group was sent to the U.S. Air Force to receive jet pilot training for much of their first year. They had been selected to keep the scientific community happy—those folks were important supporters of NASA. But the lack of flying opportunities for the scientist-astronauts created the opposite effect. Science experts understandably asked: What's the point of having a geologist among the astronauts if you only ever fly jet pilots to the moon, and never him? Pressure mounted to fly Jack. Deke placed him on our *Apollo 15* backup crew.

This would have put him on a lunar landing with Dick Gordon on *Apollo 18*. However, the program was cut back, so it would end after *Apollo 17*. The complaints began anew. Jack was bumped up one flight, to Gene Cernan's crew, and gained the very last seat on the very last mission.

With *Apollo 15, 16*, and *17*, we were getting as far away from test-piloting as we could. All three crewmembers on each mission had observational tasks to perform that had nothing to do with flying; they had to do with geology. In the meantime, we trained pilots to be scientists and trained scientists to be pilots. The scientist-astronauts excelled in helping us prepare.

As part of our backup crew, Jack naturally played a big part in Dave and Jim's geology training. He was on all our field trips, helping everybody, trying to get Dave and Jim squared away, and making sure they were superbly well prepared for the lunar surface explorations.

On his own mission, Jack became the last person to date to set foot on the moon, and naturally he found many of the most interesting lunar samples ever recovered. Some of them appear to date from early in the moon's formation and suggest that the moon once had its own magnetic field. He and Gene Cernan traveled farther on the surface than any other mission. Jack spotted and sampled a patch of orange and black glass beads that had never been seen on the moon before. He also took the best photo of the entire Earth from space, one that is still reproduced widely today.

Jack was a good pilot, a very competent astronaut, and an extremely impressive instructor with a vast knowledge of geology. In my opinion, he is the only lunar module pilot who really paid for his trip.

The last photo of a human on the moon is a shot of Jack standing with the American flag behind him. I wonder who the next person to have their photo taken on the surface will be—and what flag they will be next to.

1. High school years in Michigan. Courtesy of the Al Worden estate.

2. My delight at becoming an astronaut here in 1966 is very evident. Courtesy of NASA.

3. The *Apollo 15* crew of Jim Irwin, Dave Scott, and me. Courtesy of NASA.

4. The Saturn V rocket I flew into space. Courtesy of NASA.

5. Getting into my space suit, ready to fly to the moon. Courtesy of NASA.

6. On my way to the moon. Courtesy of NASA.

7. Orbiting alone around the moon. Courtesy of NASA.

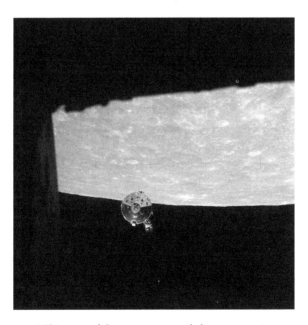

8. Flying around the moon gave me a whole new perspective
on the universe. Courtesy of NASA.

9. The distant crescent of Earth was always a stirring sight. Courtesy of NASA.

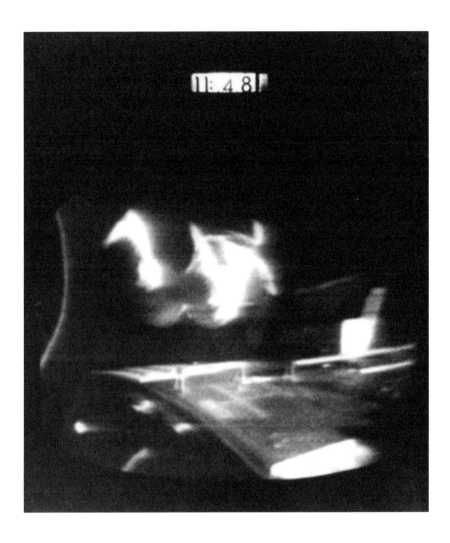

10. Between the moon and Earth, I made the first ever space walk in deep space. Courtesy of NASA.

11. After my space mission, my hometown threw me a wonderful parade.
Courtesy of the Al Worden estate.

12. By 1975 I'm living near San Francisco and looking very bohemian. Courtesy of NASA.

13. Celebrating *Apollo 11*'s fiftieth anniversary in July 2019. Courtesy of Mark Usciak.

5

The Other Twelve

Twelve astronauts walked on the moon. Less remembered are the other twelve—myself included—who traveled to the moon but did not land.

Apollo 8 and *10* journeyed to the moon as test flights before the first landing attempt. *Apollo 13* planned on landing, but, well, you've seen the movie. For the other missions, two people landed while one person orbited the moon solo, conducting science experiments and looking after the one ship that could take all three astronauts home.

These are my peers. And my peer group is shrinking—no question about it. There's a sense of realism about it. I mean, we're all getting older. But I think more about my class from West Point passing away than I do about the guys I was in the space program with. We astronauts came together as a group more in the last few years than we ever did in Houston.

You see, when I went to West Point, my whole class worked as a team. We did everything as a class. So there was a deeper understanding and knowledge and friendship with those guys. There was a sense of camaraderie when flying in a fighter squadron too. Nobody was scrambling for position; we were all simply trying to get the job done.

Getting to test pilot school can be a lifetime's crowning achievement for some. If you don't take that final step, what you do at test pilot school is absolutely the top of the ladder. But there was one step further—space. Most of us would have been really happy to just test airplanes. But when you get a chance to go into space, that's something beyond expectations.

When we astronauts were selected to go down to Houston, I think we all approached it as individuals. There was no feeling of, "This is my group." The general feeling was more one of wanting to make a spaceflight, and we were going to do it by showing that we were better than all the other guys in the group. So I never had a sense that there was a team.

Only now, decades later, have we started to relate: "Hey guys, we had a lot of fun back then, as a group." But I don't recall it at the time. We were there, we knew each other, we did some things together, but mostly we operated as individuals. Only after the competition was over could we really relate. When it's all gone, when it's done, and there's nothing you can do about it—that's when you sort of come back together again.

That's not to say some of the people I'm about to describe to you are not some of my best friends. In fact, some of them I regard as the finest people I've ever known. Let me tell you about them.

Apollo 8

Frank Borman

I know he's a colonel, but I call Frank "the General," because he always acted like one. He was official, straightforward, and businesslike. There was not a lot of nonsense with Frank—no fun and games. I think he's probably still that way.

The real deal, an astronaut's astronaut, Frank was clearly in control and professional in his approach. Given the responsibility to command *Apollo 8*, the first mission to the moon, he was very efficient. He cut everything unnecessary out of the flight plan, did the mission, and came back. His thinking was, if you go to the moon, does it make a difference whether you go around it ten times? Going around the moon was the important thing. Doing it many times wasn't important, as long as you went around at least once.

Apollo 8 was only the third time the enormous Saturn V rocket flew—and the first time with people on top. Some thought it was too early to fly astronauts, especially to send them all the way to the moon. I think it was gutsy, but it was also a testament to the people who had designed it. Frank decided to take the chance, and it turned out to be the right choice. I don't know if it would always be right, but it turned out to be a good one then. I suspect that much of Frank's decision was based on the solid engineering that went into it. He was willing to take the risk.

He attended West Point before I did and taught there after I left. It's part of why he is a natural leader. Back in the mid-1970s there was a test-cheating scandal at West Point. There was a hue and cry in Congress that the honor system was too tough. They wondered if West Point should lighten it and think of something different, so they formed a committee. Frank was chosen to head it, and he absolutely stonewalled the idea. He made sure the honor system stayed in place. His bottom line on that was that if we can't uphold an honor system at West Point, then we can't do it anywhere. That won the day.

When we had the *Apollo 1* fire at the Cape in 1967 that killed the crew, NASA formed a reconstruction committee. I was on the committee, and Frank led it. They always put Frank into these leadership positions because Frank was unique in a couple of ways. He was forceful and allowed no bullshit. Frank would listen carefully to everybody's input. He did not push his ideas on everybody else. He was very receptive to ideas and talk around the table. Then he'd make a decision. And that was it. No arguing. You didn't argue with Frank. I think that was the only way we could move on from the tragedy, because we had to move fast and get things done. We couldn't just do committee action stuff. There had to be somebody in charge. He was definitely in charge, and everybody knew it.

Frank is now in his nineties. And yet when I saw him at the Oshkosh air show a few summers ago, he flew his own airplane in. He left early, however, because he will only leave his wife Susan for a day or two. She requires full-time nursing care, and he is devoted to her. He's determined to see that she's taken care of.

Down-to-earth and efficient, a no-bullshit guy, Frank was a great leader.

Jim Lovell

I like Jim a lot. We work really well together and are good friends. He's always been very pleasant and supportive. He does the best he can to support the space program and tries to get to a lot of events. Everywhere I go, Jim's there.

Jim captured the imagination of the media when Tom Hanks turned his book about his *Apollo 13* command into a movie. It's a good book, and the movie is terrific. Both did extremely well. If you go to the visitor center at the Cape and many other places, the person you'll see talking in the display videos will be Jim. Everything at the Cape has Jim Lovell's stamp on it. He's very much a public figure. He built a nice restaurant just outside Chicago that he ran for a number of years. He does a lot of work with the Chicago planetarium and also with the local science museum. A lot of his space stuff is there. He's a great spokesperson for the space program; he was chair of the Astronaut Scholarship Foundation for several years before I took over.

Jim was selected in the second group of astronauts, and those guys got to fly as much as they liked. Jim was very much in the top of the rotation when flights came along. He was the first person to fly in space four times, and the first to go to the moon twice, on *Apollo 8* and then on *Apollo 13*. The media made a big issue out of *Apollo 13*. Jim did very well on that mission, although it was seen by a lot of people as a failure. What people didn't understand was, yes, we had a failure during the flight, but the genius of *Apollo 13* and the system we had to work with was that we got the crew back. In my mind, it's one of the most successful flights in the program. We had a major failure on the way to the moon, and yet we were able to recover it and get those guys home safely. It was probably the most important flight of the Apollo program. I think Jim deserves everything that's come his way because of it, because it was really chancy. Jim's crew had to do a lot with tape and cardboard and all kinds of things to keep the oxygen system working, but they made it work.

Jim went into the business world soon after he retired from NASA. He worked for a telephone company down in Houston; as a matter of fact, one of my daughters worked for him for a long time.

Jim is a truly good soul. I have a close relationship with him. Jim says what he needs to say, doesn't embellish it, and doesn't get emotional about it. I think his impact is better that way.

Bill Anders

Bill is another straight, true, honest guy, much like Frank Borman. We've been friends for a long, long time. I've known Bill and his wife, Valerie, since 1955, long before the space program. Bill and I both graduated that year from different military academies—me from West Point, him from Annapolis. Then we both joined the air force and went through pilot training together that year. Like me, he went into the Air Defense Command after that. We've kept in touch ever since.

Bill enjoys playing the role of a no-nonsense guy. He likes to be the gruff General LeMay type. He's always been that way. He likes to tear you a new one, but he does it with a smile. I'll let you in on a secret—he's not that way underneath. He's got the biggest heart in the world.

Bill was a pilot but not a test pilot. NASA selected him in 1963 as more of a scientist type; he was an expert nuclear engineer. With his background, I think he was a natural. He had a lot of prior contact with the guys who were responsible for selecting astronauts. He's never been short on words, nor on making connections. But he was selected because of his capability, not because he was trying to be friendly. Bill's always done his own thing and gone his own way. He has earned everything he's done; he's not beholden to anybody. I think that independence was part of what attracted NASA to him.

Bill flew to the moon on *Apollo 8* and left the program soon after to become chair of the National Aeronautics and Space Council. The guys who got out of the program fast snagged some really good jobs. We didn't really do much together after that, because he was off in a different direction. But when you've always been friends, you don't have to do a lot together.

Bill had this fancy job, and yet I can remember visiting him and Val at their house over in Virginia. He was fixing up his basement, hanging drywall. Bill did a lot of stuff like that. He never became high and mighty and has never been afraid of getting his hands dirty. These days, he's likely to be covered in engine oil from working on one of his many vintage airplanes.

Bill's star kept rising. He became the U.S. ambassador to Norway and then took increasingly high-level positions at General Electric, then Textron, until he became the chair of General Dynamics. Bill is a solid guy who makes good business decisions, and he made those companies a lot of money in the process.

He continues to tell people exactly what he thinks, and he has been very helpful when needed. When we were both inducted into the Astronaut Hall of Fame in 1997, the display was going to include an article about the *Apollo 15* postal covers. He demanded they take it out and even donated some money to see that it happened.

Bill is a strong personality, a good friend, and—as much as he wants to keep it hidden—a sweetheart.

Apollo 10

Tom Stafford

Tom is a thoughtful guy. He took great exception to how I was treated following the postal-covers incident surrounding my flight. He's the guy who really pushed me hard to write my book *Falling to Earth*, because he had definite feelings about guilt and innocence. That's the kind of guy Tom is. We're good friends, and I like him a lot.

Tom gets stuff done. He is a very detail-oriented guy. He's also a powerful guy, with important friends in government and the military. He is hugely influential in the space program, too, going back to his earliest days at NASA.

He had to deal with the power base of the Mercury guys, such as Al Shepard, and he did it well.

He was a highly respected test pilot at Edwards even before he got to NASA. I'd heard legendary stories about his quick thinking and piloting skill before I went to Houston. But I think his influence was mostly due to his personality. He's just a natural leader. You can take any group of nine people and usually pick out who the leader's going to be. In Tom's group, that was him.

I had hundreds of discussions with Tom when I was an astronaut, and I never got the feeling he was pulling rank. He talked eye to eye, as an equal. What he said always made so much sense, so we all listened to him. So he was a natural kind of guy to be in a leadership position. Not because he insisted on it, but because of the way he is.

Tom flew twice during the Gemini program. He then commanded *Apollo 10*, swooping over the landing site Neil Armstrong would aim for a couple of months later. By the time he flew his fourth and final mission, 1975's Apollo-Soyuz joint flight with the Soviets, I was long gone from NASA. I didn't follow the flight at all; I was avoiding anything to do with space at that point. I thought the international mission was a purely political project, and I was not sure at the time it was a good thing. Yet history has shown that it did help the relationship with Russia, thanks, I believe, to Tom Stafford and his Soviet counterpart, the Soyuz commander Alexei Leonov.

Alexei is an icon of the space program. He stayed best friends with Tom Stafford. They were together a lot—Tom in Russia, Alexei in the States—right up until Alexei died in 2019. Tom had elected to stay in the U.S. Air Force after his NASA career and worked his way up to a high position at the Pentagon. But then he took a different approach. I think he felt the best thing he could do was to act as a lightning rod, and so he made numerous contacts in Congress.

When Tom retired from the air force in 1979, he maintained all his contacts. He formed a consulting company and does a lot of work keeping that line open to Russia. He's extremely knowledgeable in what's going on over there and how to get things done. He's been the main liaison between the United States and Russia during all these years. He knows everybody over there. And I think everyone here understands that, so they go to Tom when they need something. He's very friendly with congresspersons and senators, and when he talks to them, they listen, because he has been right most of the time. Tom's been remarkably influential in getting Congress to pass space-related bills.

He was able to make those connections even during the tension of the Cold War, due to the genuine personal friendships he made during his Apollo-Soyuz mission training. They were closer ties than he'd had to create solely for the job. I think he realized he was in a unique position to do this. He'd made enough spaceflights. He was well known here and in Russia, and Alexei was his best friend. Tom had the opportunity, he had the mentality for it, and he had the contacts to make it happen. After the tenth anniversary of Apollo-Soyuz in 1985, Tom renewed and deepened those friendships.

I bet he travels two hundred days a year. He's always going somewhere. That's what makes Tom so valuable to everybody. If you need him, he's there. If you want something done, he's there. If you want something from Russia, he's there. He's got his finger in lots of different pies. In 2003 he and his wife even adopted two Russian boys, raised them well, and got them into good colleges.

He's very soft-spoken. You never get the impression that he is aggressive, but when he says something, people listen. Tom's a pretty unusual guy and probably the most powerful person the space program has ever had in terms of making things happen. He works hard to see that the right things get done, instead of looking for opportunities for himself. He doesn't need those. His reputation is already watertight.

Apollo 11
Mike Collins

Mike's a very solid guy. He does his thing and doesn't get involved in much. You don't see a lot of Mike in public. He is certainly not making a public spectacle of himself like some others do.

Mike and I were at West Point at the same time, but he was in the class a few years ahead of me. I never knew him there. I didn't meet Mike until I went out to Edwards. There is no question that he was a superb flier. I won't say he was the chief test pilot, but he was basically the one everybody elected as "the good test pilot." They used to have this old beat-up Model A Ford vehicle out at Edwards that they had pieced together. I was told that they'd elect somebody each year to get that Model A, because they decided he was the best pilot. Mike drove that Model A for a year, so clearly he was well thought of.

I followed Mike's career closely, because he was doing what I wanted to do. Then, of course, he got into the space program.

By this point, Mike Collins was my role model.

Mike was on the selection committee when I applied to NASA three years after him. I was glad to see him on the panel when I interviewed. I'm convinced that Mike was instrumental in getting me into the program. He later told me I was number one on his list. I still don't know why.

Mike has a subtle kind of humor. It's always of a positive nature. I don't think he ever puts anybody down. He's a well-rounded guy. He paints, he writes, and he fishes. God bless him—he's really quite an outstanding individual.

I was one of three in my selection group assigned quickly to assist with a forthcoming mission. This put me ahead of the game in getting a flight. Again, Mike Collins told me that was deliberate. I believe I owe a lot to him.

Mike was the worker in his astronaut group. He was quiet. His attitude was like mine—do your job, do it well, and you'll be okay. A really smart, astute guy, he seemed more aware of the Astronaut Office planning than most. I think he was close to Deke Slayton, but he did his own thing. You never saw him cozying up to anybody; he was always the guy who did his job and worked with his crew. I think Neil Armstrong had a big hand in this. Neil was the same way, and I believe it had an effect on Mike.

Of the *Apollo 11* crew, I came to know both Mike and Neil quite well. From what I saw, those two grew really close over the decades, because they were the same kind of people.

None of the *Apollo 11* crew flew in space again. Mike had the opportunity to command his own moon landing, had he stuck around. But I think when the crew came back from the moon, they recognized their place in history and said, "You know, what more can we do? We've done our thing. Why dilute it by sticking around?"

Mike is humble, and he's a great speaker. His talks are wonderfully informative. After he left NASA, he had a steady job as director of the National Air and Space Museum. Mike did phenomenal work there. He had me up there during those years, giving talks and reading poetry. I have the feeling Mike has always valued who I am, just as much as I value him.

You don't hear much about Mike in the media. For a long time, he lived not too far from me in Florida, but I appreciated his wishes for a quiet life. I never bother anybody if they don't want to be bothered. I'm not really into hounding people with emails and stuff; I just don't do that. But I had a long talk with him after his wife, Pat, died. We commiserated with each other, because it was the same year my wife Jill died. Pat was great. She and Mike had a really special thing going between them. She was really nice, and they were bonded for life. I am glad Mike and I could be there for each other in that tough year.

He's still my hero. Absolutely.

Apollo 12

Dick Gordon

Dick Gordon was my best friend. He looked like a movie star. He was one of the friendliest, most fun-loving guys I've ever met. And he was also really good at what he did. He had an absolute, innate ability to understand the systems he worked with and how to control them. Dick was outstanding at flying both airplanes and spacecraft.

I spent a year and a half with Dick, basically living with him. We didn't fly in space together, but we flew all over the country. I was his backup for the *Apollo 12* mission, and we sped back and forth from Houston to Downey, California, all the time in a T-38 jet. So we were working on our own a lot, unless there was something that required the whole crew, such as a spacecraft test. In all our time together, not once did we have a disagreement about anything.

I felt very close to Dick, right from the start; we always had fun when we were together. We'd have long conversations while flying out to Los Angeles about all kinds of random stuff. We'd land, jump in our rental cars, and race down to Downey. He'd see something, and I'd say, "Hey, that looks like great fun; let's do it!" That's the kind of relationship we had.

I looked up to Dick a lot, and it's probably one reason why we got on so well. But we were also similar personalities who both saw things a certain way.

Dick was an unusually hard charger at work and at play. He pursued both with the same kind of enthusiasm and energy. I mean, he was *the* guy. Everybody loved him. I think he was probably better liked than anybody else I knew back then, because he was always friendly to everyone. When I first started working with Dick, he immediately treated me as an equal. We became instant friends. I never felt any competition with him and never felt as if he acted like he was better than me because he was going on an earlier flight. We were just two guys going in an airplane somewhere to get some work done. There was an immediate rapport between us.

I think the thing that really made me like him was his sense of humor. He was always so upbeat and positive. Dick was unusual, in that he had no enemies I know of. He was so easy to get along with. He found joy in just about everything, even if it was a mistake. He'd simply laugh it away and have fun with it—that was the way Dick approached life.

He was a really hard worker. Dick would never give up on anything; he just pushed his way through each task, no matter how much time it took. Dick was really serious when it came to getting it right. I think being on that Apollo crew with Pete Conrad forced him to pay extra attention to what he did. Being with Dick as long as I was, I developed some of the attitudes he had. I tried to keep things on a lighthearted level, even though we were working hard. He was a great mentor.

He should have been the commander on *Apollo 17*—no question about that. He was so qualified and so good. It's wrong that he never got his own mission to command. The closest he got was as backup commander for my mission, *Apollo 15*. But I never got a sense that Dick was only doing the backup job to get another flight. Dick was a trouper. He seemed delighted to be on the backup crew. Obviously, he would have loved to command a flight. It didn't happen. But you have to put in the long, hard work as a backup crew to get the chance of another prime crew. That is just part of the story.

In the late 1970s and early 1980s I was running the Boy's Club events down in Palm Beach, and I gathered as many Apollo astronauts as I could for them. On the way home from one event, on a flight from Miami to Los Angeles, Dick happened to sit down next to a woman named Linda. She could equal his devilish humor, and more. He'd finally met his match, and they got married—for life. I often reminded him, "You wouldn't even know her if it hadn't been for me. I facilitated that."

I worried about him later in life. He was not in good health, and by then he was also taking care of Linda, who was in even worse condition. He was aging fast. Two unhealthy people trying to take care of each other is never good. Once Linda died, Dick didn't last long. I knew that was coming. Dick was pretty tied to her. He'd had a duty to perform, and he kept doing that, making sure he stayed alive to care for her. He was not going to give up. But once Linda went, he could be at peace himself. In one of our last phone conversations, he told me what a wonderful life they'd had together and how good it had been. I think he was ready to go.

When Dick died in 2017, less than two months after Linda, it was the passing of a real giant of the program. Because he was such a fun guy who loved to party, I don't think many people really understood how good Dick had been at his job. He was a wonderful combination of highly competent pilot and astronaut. He knew the systems; he knew everything,

Dick was full of the devil. A lot of fun. But he got the job done. He made the job fun.

Apollo 13

Jack Swigert

Jack was a screwball. He had a party at his house every weekend. One of the few bachelor astronauts, he had crazy ideas about what this meant. He chased every woman in sight. He thought that if he bought a girl a hamburger, then she was supposed to take him to bed. He spent a lot of time in Miami, where Eastern Airlines had a flight attendant school, so I guess the odds were pretty good for him with all those girls. He'd get a date with a girl, pick her up, and then ask her to buy gas for his car, because he didn't have any money. That was his attitude; Jack was really different.

I knew Jack inside and out. I knew all his foibles and the things he did as a lifelong bachelor. But I really liked Jack. He was the perfect engineer.

We joined the astronaut team in the same group. Jack was already well thought of, having test-flown the Rogallo wing, a system for landing a spacecraft with hang glider–like wings. Within our first year, we suffered the *Apollo 1* fire at the Cape. Jack and I were assigned to work on the spacecraft rebuild and reevaluate all the materials inside the command module. I spent a year and a half in California with Jack doing that.

Jack was fun, but he was also really good at what he did. He was really disciplined. We worked on a complete review of everything inside the spacecraft, replacing anything flammable with some other material, such as Beta cloth. We had weekly meetings with the manufacturer, going over changes such as the spacecraft's hatch redesign. We put a lot of time and effort into it. It was a long process, taking us months to figure out what needed to be done. It was such a shame, a real tragedy, what happened with the fire. You hate to have people killed in the program like that. But because of their sacrifice, all the subsequent flights became much safer.

The system engineers at North American, the manufacturer, created the first draft of a checklist of malfunction procedures for a crew to follow if things went wrong in flight. These procedures were troubleshooting logic diagrams, which were used in conjunction with a spacecraft systems schematic book. It was a very complex business. The engineers sent the procedures to the flight controllers in Houston, who then massaged them from their standpoint. Jack and I subsequently went through them line by line back in California. We found a ton of mistakes, due, I assume, to the fact that they were written down based on the schematics. What Jack and I then did was to test the procedures on real spacecraft at the manufacturer and change them to reflect the way the systems actually worked. It was a detailed and arduous task, which we stuck with until everything worked properly. It took us a long time to perfect them. By the end of the job, Jack and I were close friends. He was very good at that task. Whatever else you've heard about Jack Swigert and his personal life, I must tell you he was one dedicated guy, a hard worker, a good thinker, and a really good engineer.

Serendipitously, a couple of years later Jack found himself placed on the *Apollo 13* mission only three days before launch. Ken Mattingly, the prime crewmember, had been exposed to German measles, although he turned out to be fine. Then an in-flight explosion occurred. Jack, who knew those malfunction procedures so well, was a great talent to have aboard the mission. I had my heart in my throat throughout that entire flight, thinking of Jack.

I had a number of conversations with him after the flight. Because we had worked together on spacecraft procedures so much, we were both concerned that a normal procedure might have caused the explosion in the oxygen tank. The tank blew after Jack, in a normal sequence at a specified time of flight, initiated the fans to stir the cryogenic oxygen. One of the real issues with carrying oxygen during the flight was to make sure it never liquefied. If that happened, the oxygen would form a ball of liquid and float to the center of the tank, where we could never get it out for use. That is why the oxygen was kept in a cryogenic state, or in a dense cloud, and why it was stirred at certain times, to make sure it stayed in that condition. Then, to get the oxygen out, all we had to do was apply electrical voltage to the heaters in the tanks, causing the oxygen to expand and flow through the lines for use.

What finally came out of the investigation was that the tank had a built-in failure caused by the manufacturer, which had never been discovered by the technicians or the safety inspectors. Jack was in no way responsible for the explosion.

Like me, Jack ran for Congress after he left NASA. Unlike me, he won a seat. However, before he could be sworn in, he died of cancer. He was only fifty-one. He died ten years to the month since the last Americans had returned from the moon. He was the first of us twenty-four lunar voyagers to pass away.

Jack was a really good friend. He made me laugh and was a hell of a good engineer.

Fred Haise

Fred was test-flying jets at Edwards around the same time as I was, but he was doing it as one of NASA's civilian research pilots. When he and I were selected as astronauts, it was clear he was already highly respected as one of "the guys." I think that's why he was given such early flight assignments. He was a star in our group. NASA put him on the backup crew of both *Apollo 8* and *11*, and then he flew to the moon on *Apollo 13*. He and Jim Lovell were supposed to land. No such luck.

Fred saved *Apollo 13*. That's my opinion. I think Fred provided the glue that kept everything together and made sure the crew did the right thing. I believe he was absolutely the best-prepared guy on the mission.

The crew's survival depended on the lunar module. I think that's why Fred was so important; he was the guy who knew the spacecraft best. He got pretty sick from being so cold out there. Without any power, there wasn't any heat inside that vehicle, so it got pretty icy. But Fred was the brains of the crew; he stayed calm, talked the others through the procedures, and did things the right way. He really knew what he was doing. I'm not sure *Apollo 13* would have been so successful if Fred had not been on the flight—I think he was that good.

Fred's a really smart guy. But he's also extremely friendly and considerate. He's nothing like the fighter-jock stereotype. You can't imagine a nicer man.

Fred never fraternized with the management. He was his own guy—quiet, industrious, respectful, and extremely good at what he did. Even today, Fred is really good at what he does.

He had a second chance to land on the moon, as he was in line to command *Apollo 19*. But then budget cuts shortened the program. So Fred moved over to help develop the space shuttle. He test-flew the space shuttle *Enterprise* off the back of a Boeing 747, gliding it down to land on an airstrip. Making the very first landing of a space shuttle was a huge coup for his test-piloting career. Fred could have stuck around and flown a shuttle into orbit, too, but he chose instead to jump ship and work over at Grumman, the folks who built the lunar module. He rose high in management there during the next couple of decades.

I wasn't surprised he did so well in the business world. He's a really organized, logical guy. He can break a problem into its simplest components, tackle them one at a time, and get the problem solved.

You'd never know Fred was so big in the space program if you talked to him. He's just a down-to-earth, nice fellow. Other folks live off being an astronaut. Not Fred. He loves talking about being a grandpa. He's a loving family guy and stays close to home taking care of his wife.

Fred's got a new job, one he does out of love and conviction. He spends a lot of time and effort working on the Infinity Science Center in Mississippi. He lives close enough that he can drive over there and help them build a world-class space museum. Few other Apollo astronauts are going to leave such a remarkable permanent legacy. I am really proud of him. Not long ago, the center acquired and restored the enormous first stage of a Saturn V rocket for its display. Coincidentally, it was planned for use on *Apollo 19*—Fred's canceled mission.

I don't keep in touch with too many of the Apollo guys these days. But I do yak at Fred once in a while. We bounce stuff back and forth now and then. I think he is an exceptional guy.

Apollo 14

Stu Roosa

Stu was one of my students at Edwards. I was in a really strange position out there. When Chuck Yeager asked me to come and teach, he wanted me to teach advanced Aerospace Research Pilot School—a course I hadn't been through. There was a class already in progress. I was certified as a test pilot but had not been through what was considered the upper level of the school. I actually became part of the class while instructing at the same time. We had a pretty happy class altogether, and Stu was one of the leading students in it.

Stu was a good ole boy with an Oklahoma drawl. He was a very gregarious guy—a redheaded former smoke jumper, trained to put out forest fires, with a lot of flying experience. He was a hell of a good pilot. Stu collected people around him. Not because they could do anything for him, but because people gravitated to him. He was just fun to be around. He would take a bunch of the guys and go climbing up Mount Whitney. He always set up those kinds of adventures. The guys would come back with stories of how high they climbed and all the beer they drank.

We used to have great parties every week out at Stu's house. The parties were usually there, because he always had the most beer. Those folks drank a *lot* of beer. The wives were there, too; we would all mix it up, laugh, and tell stories. Those were good times. Stu's wife, Joan, was a good ole southern gal, always right in the thick of it when the parties were going on. Those gatherings ran very late at night, but since it was on-base housing, nobody paid us any attention. The cops never came. Stu was a crazy man. We were really bad—we'd burn stuff out on his front lawn, in a drunken stupor. I have no idea how that ever got started or why we did it. It was pretty crazy. He threw one hell of a party.

In the classroom, he was very smart. He knew his stuff. Stu wasn't the curious type, trying to discover new things; he didn't have that type of personality. Instead, I saw him as a guy who learned what he was supposed to learn in class, and he was really good at that.

Stu was not an excitable guy when it came to his work. When he was chosen for the space program at the same time as me, I don't remember him getting excited about it. With Stu, it was just, "Hey, that's good. I'm getting selected in the space program. Okay, well, we'll move the family down to Houston and get with it." He was a very matter-of-fact guy.

In my mind, Stu was in the middle of the pack in my astronaut selection group. He was a type A guy, very opinionated and determined in what he did. He straddled the fence by being friendly with upper management but never so friendly that he forgot the other side. I was probably more on one side, because I avoided management, feeling my work ethic would get me where I wanted to go. Stu was kind of in between.

Stu was a little—different. He was a very hard worker but always had an attitude about him. Not a bad one. He'd remark, "This is the way we're going to do it." That kind of thing. There was nothing wrong with it; he just did things a little differently. I always got the impression from Stu that he was in charge. He always acted like the leader of the crowd. Even if he wasn't.

Al Shepard came back into the running, and there were some deals made so that he would fly again. He ended up as commander on *Apollo 14*. Why he and Stu got tagged together for this mission, I couldn't tell you for sure. I suspect that there were a number of unassigned guys who could do the job, but some were better qualified than others. And Stu was the most qualified guy. Shepard also got along with Stu pretty well. They both became Coors beer distributors after they left the program, so I think there was a camaraderie there between them.

Stu was the first guy who really got into orbital science during his solo time around the moon. Farouk El-Baz, our marvelous instructor, worked hard with him to know what to look for and photograph from lunar orbit. I think Farouk had a wonderful relationship with Stu and really enjoyed working with him. Stu got into it more than prior flights, and then the whole process really matured with my flight, which came next.

Stu did not have the equipment I carried. Instead, he carried the old Hycon reconnaissance camera, which he pointed out the window to take pictures. After his mission, I can remember discussing with Stu what I should look for. Not the same lunar features, because we would be in different orbits. But he had been looking at things in a more scientific way, because he had been much better prepared and equipped to analyze features from lunar orbit, so he had good insights.

Because I left Houston right after my lunar mission, I seldom saw Stu after that. I think twenty years went by before we met up again. By 1994 some of Alan Bean's moon paintings had been made into prints, and a bunch of us Apollo veterans met at a country club in Titusville to autograph them. I guess there were probably fifteen to twenty of us there.

By then Stu had changed, although he still had a can of beer in his hand. He was taking things a little easier, going a little slower, not talking very fast, and just kind of sloughing along. I was surprised he had slowed down so much.

The same year, we also met at the big air show in Oshkosh and had a great time—Stu was in good form. We had a lot of fun, although we only really came together for a stage show one night.

At the end of that year, Stu died. I didn't see that coming. He was taken very fast. I don't think there was any indication he had a problem beforehand. He was in Washington DC visiting his son and had severe stomach pains. The family took him to the hospital, and it turned out to be really bad pancreatitis. Shortly afterward, he was gone. It was very quick.

I would have trusted Stu with my life. The fact that we were on succeeding flights—hey, that's the luck of the draw. Stu and I were pretty much parallel with what we did. I was glad he flew on *Apollo 14*, and I think he did a good job. I asked him a lot of questions about it afterward. It helped me, looking at it in hindsight now. "Hey, Stu, how did this work? How did you do that? When you looked out the window and saw something, how did you describe it, and how did the pictures come out to show that? When you did a maneuver, how did that go? When you pushed a button—did it work? When you hit the attitude controller, was it easy to do it manually, or was it better to do it computer controlled?" Those are the kinds of details I talked to Stu about.

Personally, I knew Stu as a guy who was outwardly happy-go-lucky—always with a beer in his hand, always having fun—but who was inwardly really serious. He took his work seriously, and he raised his family that way too. Through all the woodsy, good ole boy mentality and demeanor, he was very good at what he did, and he made the most of it.

Apollo 15
Al Worden

Hey, that's me!

Apollo 16
Ken Mattingly

I never really understood Ken Mattingly. He's an unusual guy. Quiet, almost introverted. Secretive. I found him a touch strange.

Ken was extremely competent as an astronaut and pilot. He was highly regarded at Edwards in the test pilot school. He was a hard worker who really knew how to do what he was supposed to do. He did his job, did it well, and never said anything much to anybody. I always liked Ken, but he wasn't the kind of person you could get close to. He seemed indifferent to human interaction.

He was almost monastic; he seemed so uninterested in any of the partying or even any of the women around, despite being one of the few bachelor astronauts back when we were selected. He was the anti-Swigert in that regard. He kept very much to himself.

I initially thought he was so quiet and so reserved that he was lucky to get the astronaut job. But he was really good at it. That's why he was selected early for an Apollo mission. He even went on to command a couple of early space shuttle flights. I'd gladly have flown to the moon with him, because he was an excellent pilot and engineer. But you'd never know it, talking to him.

Only three of us—Ken, Ron Evans, and I—orbited the moon solo with a scientific instrument bay. We're also the only ones who did a deep space EVA (extravehicular activity) on the way back to Earth. We had a lot in common, so you'd think there would have been a lot of training together. There was none. After training Stu Roosa, Farouk El-Baz shifted to me, Ken, and then Ron, one after the other.

I don't remember even talking to Ken about any of it after I got back to Earth, other than some off-the-cuff conversations and suggestions. Ken was out on his own track. I fixed the procedures for the EVA before I flew, and then those two guys did it pretty much the same way as me. Ken was the kind of guy who, when you gave him a certain procedure to follow, followed it by the numbers. He was really disciplined.

Today, I think he still avoids things. He's extremely picky about what he does, and he doesn't care what you think. He values his time, and he doesn't do much in public. He retired from the U.S. Navy as a rear admiral and spent the next couple of decades in lofty positions with aerospace companies, working on space projects. He's quite verbal in Washington. I believe he's still a very highly paid consultant there—and that's fine. He's got to do what he's got to do.

I felt bad for Charlie Duke when the fortieth anniversary of *Apollo 16* rolled around in 2012. Other surviving crews got together for some kind of public commemoration. Ken didn't want to. He told Charlie that Apollo was a long time ago—almost another life. But that's exactly why we celebrate historical anniversaries, because they are long ago. Ken wasn't interested. And although the whole crew was still alive, John Young wasn't well enough to attend any events at the time. So Charlie had to celebrate their joint achievement alone.

When Ken does give a talk—and we did an event together the other year—he takes the approach that everybody should listen to him, because he's the expert. He will talk your ear off about his pet ideas for space. It's a funny combination, when he's so quiet the rest of the time. After the talk I saw the other year, he sat off by himself, working on his computer. He was done. Ken's funny that way.

Apollo 17

Ron Evans

I'm looking at the roll call of command module pilots who flew solo around the moon or, in Jack Swigert's case, planned to: John Young, Mike Collins, Dick Gordon, Jack Swigert, Stu Roosa, me, Ken Mattingly, and Ron Evans. Only Mike, Ken, and I are left. Do old command module pilots die off before everybody else? Maybe we simply fade away. But I'm not planning on it. Not yet.

Ron Evans was the definition of a nice guy. I've never heard a bad word from him or about him. He was friendly, calm, and cool. He always had a smile; I never saw Ron get upset. I liked him a lot.

I had already left Houston by the time Ron went to the moon on *Apollo 17*. I flew from NASA's Ames Research Center down to the Cape to see that last launch of a Saturn V rocket carrying astronauts. It was a very strange launch. Already scheduled as a night launch, technical delays shifted it later and later. We were all at the viewing site, eating fried chicken and drinking Bloody Marys. The longer the flight was delayed, the more we drank. By the time they finally launched, a couple of my colleagues were stumbling.

I think Gene Cernan, Ron's commander for *Apollo 17*, was smart to just let Ron do his thing as the command module pilot. It allowed Gene to focus on the lunar module and the activities on the moon's surface. Ron was the kind of guy you could trust to get on with it like that, because he was a really good aviator.

Apollo 17 was unusual—none of the crew had been test pilots. Ron was a U.S. Navy pilot who had flown combat missions in Vietnam before coming to Houston. He was selected at the same time as me. Ron did a great job on that mission, in the same role that Ken Mattingly and I had performed. He was just as good, even though he was not a test pilot.

He gave wonderful talks after he left NASA in 1977, never hard-nosed stuff. Instead, they were delivered with a soft, goofy humor.

In 1990 Ron died in his bed at home in Scottsdale. A heart attack took him. It was surprising; ostensibly, he'd been in good shape. He was only fifty-six.

Ron and I were very comfortable together, and I always enjoyed his company. I think of Ron, and I smile.

6

Earth Views

Three Apollo missions never left Earth orbit.

Two of them were important test flights. *Apollo 7* tested the command and service modules, and then *Apollo 9* checked out the lunar module—everything that would be needed to land on the moon. It made sense to check it all out in the relative safety of Earth orbit. I want to tell you about these folks who never got to the moon, because without their test work, no one would have.

The third mission I'll tell you about was the last time the Apollo spacecraft ever flew. Years after the last moon landing, after the *Skylab* space station program, the Apollo spacecraft was used once more, on the very first international mission—the Apollo-Soyuz Test Project, a docking in space with the Soviet Union.

Plus, there's one other surprise person at the end of this chapter.

Apollo 7

Wally Schirra

I was assigned to Wally Schirra when I first joined NASA; we new guys all reported to one of the senior astronauts. It was like having a flight commander in the air force, and it was a good arrangement while we found our feet.

Upon our first meeting, Wally fixed me with a serious look. "You know, Worden," he intoned, "you've got to understand something from the start. You don't count for anything around here."

Oh crap. Was this serious? Or was it a joke? I decided to take a gamble.

"Sir, I realize I am only a captain in the air force, but I know for sure I outrank a captain in the navy!"

Wally burst into laughter and told me to go and fetch him a damn cup of coffee. The ice was broken. I had just had my first encounter with Wally the fun-loving prankster. He liked me, because I enjoyed his jokes.

When our group of astronauts started work at Houston, we weren't accepted warmly by the old guard. Absolutely not. They resented us. It took a while to get over that. I figured it was the typical response any time newcomers showed up. It was different with Wally. One of the original Mercury astronauts, he and I hit it off right away; there was no conflict. He was already planning for his last flight by then, so he didn't care much about office politics anymore. He was a great guy to work under.

Wally was always a hale, hearty guy—shaking hands and slapping backs, that kind of thing. He liked to jokingly put people down a little; that was his way of doing things. Wally had a sort of Don Rickles sense of humor and a bit of an ego issue; he did not like to have folks get anything over on him. It upset him. He liked to play games on other people, but he was really sensitive to somebody playing a game on him. As part of the original Mercury Seven group, Wally had been in the spotlight so much that it had perhaps affected how he saw things. He was very much a public figure and was always competing with the other guys in the Mercury Seven—Al Shepard in particular.

While fun loving, Wally was also extremely competent at what he did. He was the consummate test pilot and also held people's feet to the fire when he did not agree with what was going on. Wally was really determined about certain things. I saw it clearly after the *Apollo 1* tragedy. The fun in Wally evaporated for quite some time. At the committee meetings for the work to be done after the fire, he made no bones about it. "This is the way we're going to do it, by God," he'd demand. "It's for crew safety. We've got to do it." It was pretty hard to get around a comment like that, when the guy felt so strongly about it. It did mean that a lot of changes were made that might not have been done otherwise.

The problem was that Wally needed to be in control, and everyone had to do what he wanted. His *Apollo 7* flight was the last he was going to make, and he pursued the same attitude throughout the mission, which did not sit well with others. All of a sudden, we saw mission control saying, "Hey, we're supposed to be controlling the flight," and Wally retorting, "No, you're not. I'm the captain of the ship. I'm up here, and I'm the one who's in charge."

That got his crewmates, Donn Eisele and Walt Cunningham, grounded. Mission control, overseen by Chris Kraft, couldn't stop them from doing what they were doing in space. But they could sure as hell stop them in the future;

they had a lot of control over that. And they did. No one from the *Apollo 7* crew ever flew in space again.

Part of it may also have been a philosophical difference between navy guys like Wally and air force guys like me. I would always be relying on the control tower for accurate information when I flew jets. But Wally had the kind of training that goes into making a guy the captain of an aircraft carrier. An aircraft carrier's out there on its own, still with radio communication, but they have to decide what to do on their own. They're not relying on somebody else to make their decisions for them. I think they get into a mode of operation such as, "You tell me what you want me to do, and let me figure it out." I don't know if air force pilots ever really get that kind of training.

After *Apollo 7* Wally went back to being the same jokester I'd known before the flight. To me, he was the role model for a space pilot, respected as the only astronaut to fly in the Mercury, Gemini, and Apollo programs. I consider him and Al Shepard to be the two real test pilots of the Mercury Seven. Wally did not take anything very seriously, except when it came to a mission. Wally and I became great friends from the beginning. And for the rest of his life, we remained that way, still playing pranks on each other.

Donn Eisele

Donn did things that seemed crazy to me. He appeared to have no limits. I still vividly remember a prelaunch party at the Cape at the Holiday Inn. After a few drinks, Donn decided to go swimming, and with a hundred people around, he just took all his clothes off—and I mean all—and jumped in the pool. Only Donn Eisele would do that; I can't think of anybody else who would.

Donn broke a lot of unspoken rules. The one that impacted me the most was the issue of divorce.

If Deke Slayton sensed we were not focused on the job, he would have words with us. Not many words, but he didn't need many to convey his meaning. The cause didn't matter: girlfriends or wives, shady business deals, fast cars, fast food—pretty much anything. If it impaired our performance, Deke would have words. If it got into the papers and tarnished NASA's reputation, again, Deke would have words with us. Or worse, he wouldn't consider us for a mission. It was that simple.

My marriage to my wife Pam had been unraveling for years, with little drama and—more important to Deke—no impact on my work. So Deke didn't care about my marriage and eventual divorce, other than noting the casualty with normal human sympathy. Deke would later divorce too. He didn't judge, at least not the man. He judged the astronaut and his fitness for flight.

Looking around, I could see that there were a number of rock-solid marriages, some inexplicably so, in the astronaut corps. Others were not so lucky. Many astronauts who stayed with the program were so notoriously unfaithful, and so famous, that it was impossible to print the actual details of their private lives. Everyone knew. No one published the gossip, or the truth.

Donn Eisele's marriage was an issue, because he was so brazen about its failure. I don't know if it affected his performance, but it dented morale in the community. The perception of him among his colleagues was not good. Donn had a son with Down syndrome waiting at home who needed attention, but Donn was gone all the time. The absence wasn't unusual—none of us were home much, with the workload we had. The difference was that Donn didn't seem to care much about it. He'd backed out of his family and had a girlfriend at the Cape. Everyone knew about it, but nobody said anything to him. It was a sad picture.

I think Donn was yearning for the freedom to do what he wanted. But I also think he felt awfully guilty about not taking better care of his son. I suspect there was a conflict in Donn's mind about all of that. I couldn't tell you for sure, but it always felt like Donn was doing everything he could to get away from Houston. Whether at the Cape or Downey, he was always off doing something else. I've always had a sense that he felt ashamed about it.

Donn flew on *Apollo 7*, the first crewed Apollo mission. The flight was a remarkable success, orbiting Earth for eleven days, achieving every objective and more. Donn tested the spacecraft so thoroughly that it was considered safe enough to fly all the way to the moon on the next flight. He did wonderfully. But when he was pulled into the fracas Wally Schirra was creating during his disagreements with mission control, it seemed his astronaut career was probably done. It appears NASA management decided behind closed doors that with so many other astronauts to pick from, there was no need to deal with anyone from that crew again.

Then Donn and his wife Harriet got divorced, and he married his second wife, Susie, a week later. You never heard it spoken about, but this second misstep was what really blew it for Donn. It blew my mind too. Donn came to my office and told me he was going to marry Susie the following weekend, and he asked me to fly down to the Cape to be his best man. I tried to talk him into waiting. I urged him to get his feet back on the ground after the divorce, which the newspapers had covered, much to Deke's displeasure. I suggested he focus on his career for a year or so—to try to save it. If Susie was the one, she would wait and understand, I reasoned. But Donn seemed to take the invincible-astronaut mythology seriously and had decided that he could do whatever he wanted and get away with it. He was impetuous. He locked on to marrying Susie, and that was it.

Susie was a great woman, and they were happy. But Harriet was great too. You can imagine how the whole situation was looked at by his peers. Even the biggest philanderers, the hard partiers, and the self-absorbed egotists thought this was too much. Other guys were having affairs. Some even married their longtime girlfriends further down the road. But they kept the affairs quiet. Those were the unspoken rules we all lived under.

Donn was placed on the backup crew for *Apollo 10*, along with Gordo Cooper and Ed Mitchell. But this crew wasn't going anywhere. I think Gordo knew it, and so he revolted. He went off and raced cars. He didn't even show up for vacuum chamber runs. It was clear Donn was out. It was a little like some Mafia movie where the guy is still there but he's being shunned. Donn was theoretically ready to step in and fly to the moon at a moment's notice. In reality, as far as Houston was concerned, he was dead. He soon left.

I was separated from my wife Pam. I didn't want the same thing to happen to me. I talked it over with Deke and with Dave Scott, so they knew what was going on. Pam and I could have stayed separated until after my *Apollo 15* flight, but I didn't think that would be fair to her. So Deke told me to keep it low-key, to keep my nose clean, to not get into a public squabble about this thing, and I'd be fine. And that's the way it turned out. Deke was true to his word.

Donn Eisele broke the mold when he married Susie, but he did it poorly and was asked to leave. I was the first one in the program to get a divorce and still get a flight. After that, many other shaky marriages came unglued, and within a couple of years, few of those couples were still together.

Donn went on to have a good, happy life. He and Susie stayed together until the day he died. The other year, I was down in Fort Lauderdale to help celebrate the ten-year anniversary of a moon-rock exhibition at a library there, in memory of Donn. Many of Donn's children were there, and I saw that it was time for me to understand the second chapter of his life. After NASA, it seemed Donn had been a successful, loving father and husband. It was clear he was remembered with great affection. Even the contentious issues of the *Apollo 7* flight had long faded, leaving the magnificent engineering success of the mission.

I was glad to learn that Donn got his second act right.

Walt Cunningham

I always felt a little sorry for Walt, to be honest.

Stuck in orbit during *Apollo 7* with an outspoken commander, Walt had no way to escape the wrath that came down on the whole crew after splashdown. I don't think Walt got into the inflight arguments at all—certainly not compared to Wally and Donn. But Chris Kraft was the kind of manager who cared more about power than fairness. He liked to bring astronauts down a notch when he could. So Walt was chopped out.

Just like Donn's, Walt's was a lingering death. Walt was given other assignments. Most notably, he was asked to head up the *Skylab* branch, getting NASA's first space station in shape. He could have fully expected to command a mission. But when it became clear he was simply a placeholder until others came back from the moon and took those seats, Walt got the message and got out of there. That's how Chris operated, time and again. He didn't fire you—he simply ruined your career and left you in limbo, until you wised up, sometimes after years of waiting for another flight that never came.

Walt had been brought into the program in 1963 as more of a science type. He was a military fighter pilot who'd served over in Korea, but NASA wanted him most for his work in physics. He's an interesting guy who designed the house he built in Nassau Bay when he came to Houston. It was an unusual house, very modern, with lots of glass. That's the kind of person Walt was—a detail-oriented guy who would really dig in to architectural stuff and figure it all out.

Walt and I hung out together much of my time in Houston. We'd go waterskiing every weekend. We were really competitive on things outside the program, especially handball, which we'd play almost every day. Mike Collins was better than either of us; he was the clear champion. But Walt and I would often jostle for second place. Well, he would jostle. Walt was a good player, but generally, I beat him. As the top guys, the three of us were always challenging each other. Once in a while, I would beat Mike Collins—but not often. He was just too good.

Today, Walt enjoys being seen as a tell-it-like-it-is guy. He has tempered his outlook a little as he's grown older—but not much. He's got an email list that must be a mile long, and he sends something out just about every day. He can be brash and outspoken, and this can be a little bit of a problem, because Walt all too often presents himself as the guy who knows. There are subjects in science and politics he is very forthright and blunt about. But Walt is not a middle-of-the-road guy; he's either all one way or all the other. I just take what he says with a grain of salt, and he's fine with that.

Walt and I are at events around the world together a lot, and we are still friendly.

Apollo 9

Jim McDivitt

If you go to my hometown of Jackson, Michigan, less than three miles from the farm where I grew up, you'll find James A. McDivitt Street.

McDivitt Street. Not Al Worden, the guy who was born and raised in Jackson. Jim McDivitt, from Chicago, two hundred miles away around the southern coast of Lake Michigan, over in the next state.

What the hell?

Here's what happened: His folks moved to Jackson when he attended community college there. He was only in college in Jackson for two years. But the city claimed him, of course. When he got back from flying in space on *Gemini 4* in 1965, they threw him a huge parade. "It's great to be back," he told the press that day. "I've been looking forward to coming home for a long time."

Home? He stole my town!

I could almost forgive him, except for what he did next.

When I joined NASA, the year after his Gemini mission, we soon worked out that our parents lived three blocks apart. Naturally, they quickly got to know each other. My mother called me Sonny when I was young, a nickname that had stuck with me until I went to West Point. Thankfully, I got rid of the name then and hoped it would be gone forever. But somewhere in the conversations between the two families, Jim found out.

The next time I was walking down a hallway at work, a voice rang out, "Hey! Sonny! Sonny Worden!"

Jim and his wife, Pat, called me Sonny for the rest of my time at NASA. He's still laughing about it.

Within my first year at NASA, I was assigned to the support crew for what would be Jim McDivitt's Apollo command mission. It was named *Apollo 2*, and I did that for a month, until the *Apollo 1* fire changed all our plans. But by late 1967 I was back on Jim's support crew for what was now going to be *Apollo 8*, which then became *Apollo 9*. Jim asked me to focus on the docking system between the command module and the lunar module. I went through all the tests with the docking system, out at Downey and then down at the Cape. The system had never been flown, and we had to certify it in the factory. That was my big responsibility.

Astronauts were assigned to crews with the concurrence of the commander for that flight. I know Jim McDivitt was really happy to have me on his support crew. Dave Scott was the command module pilot on Jim's crew, so Dave also saw how I could work. When Dave was given his own crew, it was not a big step for him to say, "I want Al Worden on my crew with me."

I thoroughly enjoyed working for Jim on *Apollo 9*. He was a lot like Pete Conrad, very capable of doing what he was doing, but with a sense of humor that wouldn't quit. He and Pete both liked to tell stories, to laugh, and to be with people. Jim's a people person. He made it enjoyable to work for him. He always got his point across without being demanding or pounding his fist on the table. Jim was really easy to work with, but he made sure it was done his way. He even made it enjoyable for people to do it his way. He helped me a lot. So I've always liked Jim; we've been good friends for a long time now.

Apollo 9 was the test flight of everything that would be used for a moon landing; only, it was tried out in Earth orbit. It was the first crewed flight of the lunar module, which meant all kinds of intricate rendezvous and docking maneuvers. In other words, it was a test pilot's dream mission to command—plus, Jim had a really good crew to do it with. Jim was a good commander; he knew what he wanted to do and then how to do it. He was all business, and so everybody else got in that kind of mode. He was very decisive about things but was also really nice; he was not a hard driver or anything.

Jim was a head above most of the guys in the program, and that is probably why he became the Apollo program manager after his flight. If anyone could have turned around right after *Apollo 9* and commanded a lunar landing mission, it would have been Jim. But instead, he oversaw the whole program, including challenging situations such as *Apollo 13*.

Then he resigned from the Apollo program, because Gene Cernan was given the *Apollo 17* command position. It wasn't Jim objecting to Gene, I think, so much as they forced the decision on Jim. That was his big objection. He did not select the crews, but he was the program manager and was supposed to have a say. Jim was upset by it, to the point where he said, "I think I've had enough."

Jim had a great career in the business world after NASA and did really well. He's an exceptionally nice guy and really smart. Jim's showing his age a little, now that he's over ninety, but he's still as irascible as ever. I don't see him other than every few years, but we are still close.

Rusty Schweickart

Rusty and I should be closer than we are. In many ways, we have a lot in common.

In the early 1970s, when I had longer hair and a big mustache and was hanging out with musicians and poets in San Francisco, Rusty and I looked pretty alike. He ended up living in the Bay Area, too, with the same crowd.

Rusty and I also had strikingly similar experiences in space. When he was in Earth orbit and had a few unexpected minutes to simply gaze out at the dark abyss during a space walk, his experiences changed him. Years later, he pondered what humankind's place is, moving out into the universe. He understands—indeed, feels in his bones—that Apollo was more than a technological triumph. It was a glimpse into the future of humanity. Like me, he felt the nudge of the evolutionary step we were taking as a species into a wider cosmos. Looking back at our home planet, he understood it as never before. All of this sounds so much like my experiences on the far side of the moon, gazing out into a blaze of starlight. We should be bonded by this shared experience.

Why, then, in the 1980s—in discussions to promote world peace, of all things—did Rusty and I almost get into a fistfight?

I admit, these days I'm a curmudgeonly and occasionally crotchety old conservative. Even back in the 1970s when I was enjoying the freewheeling Bay Area, I was still conservative in my political views. That's pretty typical for an air force veteran of my generation. Rusty, however, is anything but conservative. He's pretty liberal. That's okay, because I have friends of many different political beliefs. But one day Rusty and I really butted heads. And even before we fell out, we had other little clashes.

I had a disagreement with Rusty when I was preparing for my *Apollo 15* space walk, but it had nothing to do with politics. Rusty had worked on setting up the equipment and the procedures for my EVA. From an engineering perspective, on paper, it looked great. In real life, I had doubts. I have always believed that the most important thing in engineering is keeping it simple. Rusty had studied at MIT and had an impressive background in engineering, but I felt his approach was more theoretical than practical.

We had a problem to solve. I was going to float out of the spacecraft on the way back from the moon and recover film canisters from the cameras I had been operating in lunar orbit. Rusty had been working on some complicated ways to get them back in. He'd abandoned a swing-arm idea as being too heavy and cumbersome, and he ended up instead with a complex clothesline pulley arrangement. It worked okay in tests in a swimming pool. But when I was assigned to the mission, I took a look at it and said, "We're going to be out there in free fall, so it won't be effective. I just don't think the system's going to work."

I'm a hands-on guy, and I like to check things out personally. So we tested it further. We flew simulations many times in a zero-g airplane, with me running those canisters back and forth on the clothesline to the hatch. Almost every time, the canisters would begin swaying around halfway, because you cannot pull a cord like that smoothly and evenly. Eventually, one swayed so much that it knocked a rocket thruster right off the side of the service module mock-up. The idea was hurriedly abandoned. On the real mission, I did the easiest thing—I grabbed the canisters by hand and carried them back. Simpler was better.

Rusty is an incredibly smart guy, and we often need engineers who are more theoretical than practical. This was just a difference in approach. Our big falling out came when Rusty was part of creating the Association of Space Explorers.

In the spring of 1984 he was putting this organization together with the idea of bringing spacefarers together from around the globe to share mutual perspectives. I thought, and still think, it is a great idea. Jim Irwin, Alan Bean, Ed Mitchell, Donn Eisele, and Jerry Carr were joining us too. So when we met at the Pepsi headquarters in the New York area, I was eager to assist if I could.

The organizing part of the meeting went well, I thought. But then Rusty started selling his vision of spaceflight as a peaceful enterprise where all countries with space capability would publicly identify their plans. At the time, we were still in the Cold War with the Soviets, and I knew in my heart that Russia would violate the agreement and continue on their path of nonpeaceful space applications. I believed Rusty wanted to get America to live up to full disclosure and hoped Russia would do the same. The Russians would have loved that; if America had given up on everything except peaceful purposes, this would have left the door open for them to secretly continue their military space work. I felt we'd be writing something that would help our enemy. Now, maybe this was wrong, but it's exactly what I thought at the time.

When I told Rusty that I didn't agree with his approach, he got really upset with me. We got into a face-off; in fact, we almost came to blows over it. I removed myself from the group and did not get involved in the Association of Space Explorers again for several years, until I finally attended a conference in Europe.

Understandably, Rusty and I weren't too friendly for many years after that. I avoided him for a long time. In the last few years, however, we've become friendly again. Plus, Rusty has now been working on something I can 100 percent agree with: the threat to this planet from asteroids.

What would it say about us as a species if an asteroid was heading to Earth, one that would wipe us out, and we had the technology to divert it—but we never got around to doing it? We'd be pretty dumb. Sadly, it's kind of where we are right now. We have the ability to detect dangerous rocks that could make us as extinct as the dinosaurs. We have space technology that could be repurposed to deflect the dangerous mountains of rock in our solar system. And yet we are not doing either of these things as well as we could, for the usual reasons—no governments are focusing on them and funding them enough.

Rusty has been all over the world in the last few decades, giving talks to world leaders and influential organizations, making a clear case that investing in these areas is vital for humanity's sustained future. I have to admit that he's doing some of the most important work any astronaut has done after their space career was over. I admire him for this and thank him.

What if, one hundred years from now, a huge asteroid heading directly for Earth is deflected and humanity is saved—including my own descendants—as a direct result of Rusty's tireless efforts?

This old curmudgeon is going to look pretty foolish for ever doubting him, isn't he?

Apollo-Soyuz
Vance Brand

Vance and his wife, Bev, have been friends of mine, it seems, forever. I met Vance in 1966 when he was selected in my astronaut group. Before that, he'd been an accomplished civilian test pilot. He's an easygoing, smiling, soft-spoken cowboy type, sporting a mane of long white hair these days, who looks like he'd be equally at home riding a horse through the desert as flying a sleek jet.

I like Vance. He's comfortable to be around.

Vance was a pretty quiet fellow who just did his thing, didn't create waves, and worked on whatever needed to be done. He was my backup for *Apollo 15*. And yet while Dick Gordon and I spent a lot of time together as prime and backup crewmembers for *Apollo 12*, I never got to do this with Vance. We didn't get to do simulations together. I think there was so much more expected of my role on *Apollo 15*, and I was often busy training on my own. On the occasions when Farouk El-Baz would train us both, Vance and I would go over the charts together, but I barely noticed his presence. He was such a smart guy that he just quietly soaked it all up.

Vance would have flown on *Apollo 18* with Dick Gordon, but when the lunar landing program was cut back, he moved over to the Apollo-Soyuz Test Project—the docking in space with the Soviets. He did a great job on that mission.

Vance wrote his memoir the other year. Naturally, I turned right to the section about *Apollo 15*. Vance talked about how it seemed clear I wasn't going to break my leg before the flight, so he wouldn't be required to take my place. Ever since, I have joked with Vance about how much he had wanted my legs to be broken so that he could have gone to the moon.

But what if something bad had happened to me and Vance had taken my seat? What if we had switched places?

I wouldn't have gone to the moon, but I would have had one hell of a career. After the Apollo-Soyuz mission, Vance commanded the fifth space shuttle mission, the first one to be considered operational, and then he commanded another two—the last one in 1990, almost two decades after I'd flown in space. Would I have traded one moon mission for four Earth-orbit flights? That's pretty tempting.

After his four missions, Vance made another move that would have tempted me—he went to NASA's Dryden Flight Research Center up at Edwards and got back into flying research airplanes. He did this until 2008. Although he wasn't flying in space any more, technically he was still on the astronaut list the whole time. So thirty-seven years after he backed me up on *Apollo 15*, Vance was still an astronaut. That's really impressive.

Additionally, if I had been him, I would never have been pulled into the *Apollo 15* postal-cover issue. Perhaps, in a way, it's too bad I didn't break my leg.

There's another thing I love about Vance—whenever you see him, you see Bev too. They are like a couple of pioneers, living in California's Tehachapi Mountains above the desert where Vance landed space shuttles a couple of times. Bev is the sweetest woman in the world, and the two of them do a lot of traveling together. They are like two halves of one personality; they are so beautifully connected.

Vance is a cool guy. A very competent pilot, he could easily have flown in my place when needed. When you listen to that quiet voice, you don't think he's going to be a funny guy at first. But if you listen carefully, you'll find a lot of little gems he throws out.

Just watch that he never breaks your legs.

Deke Slayton

In May 1972 I was on a geological field trip in the Southwest, supporting the *Apollo 17* mission. At seven in the morning, my hotel room phone rang. It was my boss—Deke Slayton.

When your boss calls you so early, it's generally really good, or else really bad. This time, it was bad. I was told to fly back to Houston the same day and, by the end of the week, to be gone for good.

In April 1966 I'd had a much nicer call from Deke. I had been at Edwards at the test pilot school, and he was calling to offer me the job of astronaut.

I got to know Deke well in the six years between one of the best days of my life and one of the worst.

Deke was the head of Flight Crew Operations, meaning he selected who flew in space. Our careers depended on him. But that's not why NASA had chosen him. In 1959 it had selected him as one of the original Mercury Seven astronauts.

Deke is in this chapter, however, because he made his first and only space-flight in 1975, sixteen years later, as part of the Apollo-Soyuz mission.

What happened?

In 1962, right before he was about to fly a Mercury mission, doctors grounded him because of a minor heart irregularity. Deke could have left NASA, but instead, he became, in essence, the chief astronaut. If you were NASA, trying to set up an Astronaut Office, then you had to pick somebody who had the background and the experience to do this. Deke, available because he couldn't fly, was the absolute natural pick. It was a wise arrangement. As one of us, Deke was someone his fellow astronauts trusted.

He was a great manager. Each week, he'd convene a meeting that we all attended, designed to update us all on the status of the current program. He would also use this forum to talk about any problems outside the program that might affect us. Veteran astronauts would update us all on issues they had with projects they were working on, sharing problems or concerns. Additionally, Deke handed out assignments to everyone.

Deke was a good ole boy—very straight and honest. I really liked him, and I think he did a superb job. My fellow astronauts used to gossip about the huge question looming over us all—what did it take to get on a flight? They wondered if trying to be Deke's best friend would help them. The truth is that Deke played things straight. He didn't play favorites. He was a straightforward guy, with a very conservative approach. As long as you kept your nose clean and didn't cause any embarrassment, you were fine. If you caused a problem, you'd be history. I would never argue with him, because Deke was right most of the time. He was a solid guy.

Deke didn't want us doing anything risky on a mission—no tasks we didn't need to do. He was pretty straightforward about that, saying, "Let's get the job done and not worry about other stuff." He was a pilot, not a scientist. I am sure in his mind the whole point of the program was to fly and to walk on the moon. Forget the rocks and other distractions.

By 1972, as the Apollo program was winding down, Deke was able to convince the doctors he was fine to fly. Unfortunately, as the price of doing so, Deke had to give up his job as director of Flight Crew Operations. For him, it was an understandable trade—he was finally able to fly in space. For NASA, it was a bad deal.

A few months earlier, when Deke was still in charge and saw the mess our crew had created with the postal covers, he saw it as a violation of his trust. And it was. We let him down. I think Deke would have gone as far as he could to let it go without making an issue of it. I truly believe he would not have fired me if given the chance. There were more appropriate punishments than being kicked out, and he knew it. He was a good guy. But eventually he had no choice; other, much less fair people were flexing their muscles.

The guy who was gunning for me to be fired, Chris Kraft, was the same guy who kicked the chair out from under Deke as soon as he traded in his management role for a flight into space. As soon as Chris got Deke to relinquish his job, I believe it destroyed the integrity of crew selection forever. Kraft now had all the power he wanted and immediately took the punch out of the Astronaut Office—its importance fell away in the eyes of many.

I let Deke down, and I am sorry for that. I believe NASA let Deke down by dismantling the fair system he'd built. The only bright side is that after a decade and a half of waiting and battling doctors, Deke finally got to see the glory of Earth from space.

Dee O'Hara

I've talked about all the people who flew Apollo missions. There's one other person I want to tell you about who never flew in space but is as important to the space program as anyone who did. Her name is Dee O'Hara.

We pilots never liked visiting the flight surgeons. There was never a positive outcome from a visit to the doctor. Only two things could happen: we could still be allowed to fly, or we'd be grounded. Look at what happened to Deke Slayton, for example. We never wanted to get exposed to that kind of risk. But Dee was always there, always on our side. She did the right thing by us. If I ever had a problem, I went to Dee. I didn't go to the doctor if I could help it.

Dee started out as an air force nurse at the Cape, assigned to the Mercury Seven at the start of the space program. NASA had asked for her to come and take care of the early guys, because she was the only qualified nurse around. Once she got there, they said, "Hmm, we have got a winner here. We'd better do whatever we can to keep her." So they talked her into leaving the air force and joining NASA, where she became a civil servant. She moved to Houston to set up a flight-medicine clinic. She still went back to the Cape for every launch, however, to medically check out each crewmember about to head to space. She did this with the first American-crewed spaceflight, in 1961, and ended with the first flight of the space shuttle, twenty years later.

She loved everybody and took good care of the crews. She's wonderful, and I love her. She is probably the most revered person outside of the astronaut corps for all of us guys. She took care of some serious problems some of the astronauts had, on her own, to keep them away from the authority of the flight surgeons, who could drop them from flight status. I think it all worked out;

she knew what she was doing. Guys would have some really personal medi-cal issues, and she would never tell the doctors, as long as it didn't affect the astronaut's job performance. She'd get them the right treatment and take care of whatever it was. Imagine the most personal, embarrassing medical issues you could have. You're probably imagining the right things.

Dee became really friendly with all the astronauts' wives and their kids. They went to her if they needed anything done. She was always extremely supportive and was especially close to the wives. Dee knew that a happy fam-ily was a big asset for a guy who was gone all the time, and she saw to it that they remained comfortable and unworried. She could provide counseling to them, help them through the rough spots, and take care of the kids when they got sick. Dee was really important to those families. But it wasn't an official thing—she did it on her own. That's just how she is; Dee always goes way above the job description.

So I've known Dee for a long, long time and always considered her one of my closest and best friends. We don't see each other much anymore, as we live in different parts of the country, but we're still close as far as friendship. And I bet she would say the same thing. When I left Houston in 1972 and went to Ames, I kept in touch with her. A year after I left, she was telling me on the phone how she was getting dissatisfied with Houston, because things weren't the same. There was going to be a major lull before the space shuttle started flying. So I asked her, "Well, Dee, why don't you come on out here? The people who work here are really smart and doing very advanced work. They have an experiment going on that's right up your alley. It's a bed-rest study, where they put people in bed for three weeks and see how they do, because the effects are similar to being in space." She was interested, so I talked to the Ames director. She came out for an interview, met with all the medical people, and was offered the job. Because she was such a good friend of mine, I flew to Houston and drove her out when it came time for her to move. It was in the middle of a gas crisis, and no matter which route we took, we had to wait in long lines to get fuel. It was tough—it took many days to get to California. Dee also had her dog with her—the ugliest dog I have ever seen, with teeth pointing in every possible direction. I think Dee must have taken pity on it, because she really loved that mutt. Once we got to California, she bought a nice townhouse, and she's still living in it, very happily.

Dee is an exceptional nurse but doubly exceptional in how she cares for people. She ought to be named a saint—she really should. One of life's warmest, friendliest, and most helpful people, she is also one of the best friends I've ever had in my life.

There are, of course, many other colleagues I could tell you about who almost flew during the Apollo program. Gus Grissom and Ed White, for example, died in a tragic launchpad fire before getting the opportunity to fly their mission. My good friend C. C. Williams and the talented Charlie Bassett both died in jet crashes. Ed Givens, from my astronaut selection group, was lost in a car crash. Some of these guys would have made their mark on the moon, literally. And in a way, they did. During our *Apollo 15* mission, Dave Scott gently placed that plaque into the lunar soil with the names of fourteen spacefarers who had passed away—both American and Russian. It was a fitting way to remember their sacrifice.

7

The Hoax of the Moon Hoax

Even before I left NASA, I used to get letters from people who believed the moon landings had been faked. These were the same people who believed in a flat Earth. They also wrote to me that little men came out of the North Pole in UFOs. It was easy to dismiss these ideas. But then there was one guy in particular who went into great detail to try to prove that the moon landings had been faked. He looked at flags seemingly waving on the moon, and he looked at shadow patterns on the lunar surface. He wrote a book and did a bunch of interviews about it. Of course, there are very logical explanations for all the things that he queried, but he used the facts a little differently and concluded that we never could have gone to the moon. That was in the mid-seventies, and I think that's when all the conspiracy theory talk truly began. There was a movie that came out not long after named *Capricorn One*, about NASA faking a mission to Mars. It was a good movie. But apparently some of these people thought it was a documentary.

The answer to all the theories, of course, is very simple. Of course we went to the moon. You cannot pay five hundred thousand people enough money to keep them quiet.

Do you not believe twenty-four astronauts when they tell you their stories of going to the moon and coming back? Do you think they have been brainwashed? I think it's impossible to brainwash twenty-four people.

Then there's seeing an actual Saturn V launch. There's no faking that. You see that big object going off the launchpad, and if they're not going to the moon, where are they going? Where else could they go? To a film set in Arizona? So where did they get the rocks that are not from Earth? I just think that's impossible. You can't fool that many people.

I think part of the reason a few people still have doubts is that humans only went to the moon for four short years, 1968 to 1972. We have not been back since, and that's now half a century ago. It was a very small slice of historical time. I was really fortunate to be there at the right moment and get the ride that I did. It was such a phenomenal period in our history. I wonder whether the fact that we haven't been back makes people think, "Well, if we can't do it now, how could we have done it then?"

I think the climate we lived in during the mid-1970s also had a lot to do with any misperceptions. It was the time of Watergate, so there was a deep distrust toward any official voice, especially from the government. There was an undercurrent of cynicism in the nation. We're seeing it again today, and it causes so many problems. People are polarized in their beliefs, and they were polarized back then about the value of moon landings.

This happens with any subject that we don't understand. I believe it's very easy to capture somebody's imagination if they really don't understand what the reality is. Then they'll think, "Hey, there's no way we could go to the moon and walk around on it! We just can't do that! You know, the moon is so far away. I mean, come on, we sent a six-and-a-half-million-pound vehicle off the launchpad and sent three guys to the moon? And they landed there and drove a car on the moon? Who are you kidding? We can't do that!" I think it's simple to slip into that if you don't identify and research the true story.

How we got to the moon back then was not too mysterious. But it was something that many people couldn't comprehend, because it was so far out of the realm of what they thought was doable. If you know anything at all of the mechanical side of it, you quickly conclude, "Oh, sure, we can do that, no problem." But it can be hard for others to understand what we did, so there's a kind of intellectual or mental process that they go through. They look for reasons to say we didn't do it.

But we did.

It reminds me of my experience with a supposed perpetual motion machine. When I was still working for NASA out at the Ames Center, a guy came to visit and told us he had this machine that could take us to the moon and wouldn't cost us any energy. So we had him demonstrate it. It looked like a big spider with weights on the arms. When the arms moved, the spider would move forward. Then very slowly the arms would retract, and it would do it again. So this thing would creep around the room. I thought that was very . . . nice. But the guy was uninformed. He completely forgot about friction between the machine and the floor, which allowed it to move. So for a couple of years, we would give him improvements to make, and he'd come back and do the same thing. Finally, we had to tell him one last time, point-blank, "When your machine comes in contact with the floor, there's friction that allows it to move. Out in space, you don't have that friction, so it's not going to go anywhere." I think this is the kind of thinking that leads people into believing a moon hoax. They don't understand all of it; they only know a piece. And out of that piece, they develop a whole story.

I've had a lot of people ask me questions at my public talks. They'll say, "I saw this show on TV, and the flag waved on the moon," or, "I saw a photo on a website, and some rock on the moon had a mark on it." Those misperceptions are easy to answer. There was a pole in the top of the flag, holding it out, and sometimes a hair got onto the film during the printing process. There's a very logical reason for what they saw, and when it's explained to them, they reply, "Oh, yeah! Sure, now I understand." They actually want to know. I would say those are 99 percent of the moon-hoax questions.

Then there is the 1 percent. I think the problem with those people is that they don't want to see the other side. They really want to believe what they believe, and they don't want anybody to upset that. No one is going to convince them otherwise.

So if people are really interested in talking about it, then I'll talk as long as they want. But if they're throwing questions out there just to get a reaction, then it's a very short conversation.

The worst was a guy named Bart Sibrel. He would ambush and upset astronauts such as Neil Armstrong. One day, he got me too. I was at the Kennedy Space Center Visitor Complex doing a big event with many of the other Apollo guys. This Bart guy came up with a TV camera and ABC press credentials, aimed the TV camera at me, and started talking about classified tapes proving the Apollo missions were falsified. I shook my head and told him it was total nonsense. Then he held out a Bible and asked, "Would you swear on a Bible that you actually went to the moon?"

I could see that this guy was a little bit . . . off. So I turned and stepped back to the table where people were waiting for me to sign photos. While the security people waved at him to stop, Sibrel kept insisting. I told him that I didn't feel like I had to do that, just to prove something to him. My mission speaks for itself. I was trying to sign autographs for visitors and make it a nice experience for them, but this guy wouldn't stop.

My friend Al Hallonquist, a former cop who was acting partly as security that day, was sitting behind me with my wife. Eventually, I called him over. Nobody was going to confront Hallonquist for very long, because he's a big guy. As I recall, he got more of the center's security people, and they hustled Sibrel out. He wasn't there as a TV reporter; he was just a busybody who wanted to prove something to somebody.

Not long after that, Sibrel confronted Buzz Aldrin in Beverly Hills in front of a hotel. He circled Buzz and called him a thief, a coward, and a liar. Buzz eventually had enough and punched him in the face.

Over the years, many Apollo astronauts had fallen out with Buzz for one reason or another. But when we saw that moment on the news, with Buzz defending our integrity, we cheered. For the next year or so, none of us had anything but good things to say about Buzz Aldrin.

I can't tell you how many of those crazies I have had to deal with over the decades. And when I later browsed Buzz Aldrin's memoir, *Magnificent Desolation*, I noticed he justified his actions that day by saying, "Maybe it was the West Point cadet in me, or perhaps the air force fighter pilot."

And I thought, "I was a West Point cadet too. And an air force fighter pilot. Hmm."

Maybe I will get angry enough to do the same thing someday. I doubt it, but you never know. I still think Buzz did the right thing.

In the meantime, for the people who are genuinely curious and have seen or read some misleading information, here's a final answer.

No one doubts that the Saturn V rockets launched. A million people saw *Apollo 11*'s launch with their own eyes. That rocket was going somewhere. And the Soviet Union, our Cold War enemy, had all these tracking radar devices that could follow a spacecraft out to the moon and back. The Soviets would have loved to expose any American lies and humiliate us.

So there's only one way a moon hoax theory would work—the Soviets, at the height of the Cold War, would have to be in on it with their sworn enemies.

Need I say more?

8

I Never Liked the Space Shuttle

I didn't get to stick around Houston after my *Apollo 15* flight. It wasn't my choice.

When I got back from the moon, the astronauts had already been selected for the three *Skylab* space station missions. The only other flight, Apollo-Soyuz, wasn't even finalized yet. There wasn't anything else left unless I stuck around for the space shuttle.

I was assigned to back up the *Apollo 17* crew after we got back. Of course, by then NASA had already decided that the Apollo lunar program would end with *Apollo 17*. I was asked to help out because I was well trained to step in at the last moment. But I wasn't needed in the end. In fact, I never flew in space again.

But what if things had been different and NASA hadn't cut the Apollo budget back? As I mentioned before, I might have commanded a moon landing mission on *Apollo 21*. But there wasn't an *Apollo 21*. There wasn't even an *Apollo 18*. I think it's a shame. I absolutely believe that NASA management turned chicken. The *Apollo 13* explosion spooked them. We had six highly successful landings on the moon—so what else could happen? Well, a big accident could happen. That would have happened sooner or later. You can't win 'em all. We found that out with the space shuttle, big time. The shuttles were not as safe as NASA thought they were. But back in the Apollo era, with the potential for a catastrophic accident, NASA management cut the moon landing program just as it was getting really interesting. They would have stolen money and equipment from *Apollo 15*, too, if there had been anything worth stealing.

NASA said it was because it needed to focus on designing and building the shuttle. I don't think that was the main reason. I know they diverted that Apollo money to the shuttle program, but I think there was also an element of concern that we could destroy all the good stuff we'd done by having one bad accident. We had weak management back then. It was what I call maintenance management. We already had the Apollo program planned out and scheduled. The only thing they could do was delay a flight or kill the program. So they killed the program. I think that was a testament to the lack of leadership we had at NASA at the time.

They made their choice. They killed off the greatest program of human exploration there has ever been and confined us to low Earth orbit for the next half century, maybe longer. But at least the tiny cost savings they made helped fund the space shuttle, right? No, that was another bad move. I was not a fan of the shuttle. I never have been.

The shuttle was supposed to be the next wave of exploration, making space affordable and accessible. Yet I can remember going to a NASA management meeting at Langley, in the early 1970s when I had left Houston and worked for NASA at Ames. They were working on the shuttle program. During a break, I took a walk outside with Rocco Petrone, the Apollo program manager. Rocco was a very brusque and demanding guy, but he got the job done. Nobody crossed him, because he had a fierce temper, although I always thought he was fair. We were talking about a number of subjects, and Rocco told me he was really unhappy with the design of the shuttle. During Apollo, with a Saturn booster, if we lost an engine we just kept going, as the other engines canted a little bit and kept us on track. The others were still close enough to the centerline of thrust that the vehicle could still operate. The shuttle, however, didn't have centerline thrust, which I found incredibly foolish.

With an off-line thrust, as the shuttle headed for orbit and the enormous external tank grew lighter, the center of gravity of the whole shuttle stack kept changing. The engines had to be constantly canted to compensate. To keep the whole thing balanced, the heavier liquid oxygen tank had to be placed above the much lighter liquid hydrogen propellant tank. The piping from those tanks had to withstand a lot of additional stress because of the constantly shifting forces caused by this off-balance design. Rocco and I agreed that this was all very dangerous. That was enough reason right there for me not to like the shuttle. When Rocco understood that NASA was going to do it anyway, he resigned. He did not want to be involved in something that could be very bad for NASA.

In my opinion, the shuttle had several other serious safety issues. There was no way out if they had a launch abort. They could talk all they wanted about flying back to the launch site or landing at some remote field, but those predictions were never practical. The shuttle also had major problems with its heat shield and the fragility of the tiles. They kept falling off, even before the first shuttle flew.

Rocco worked away from the space industry for a long time, but he eventually came back to work at Rockwell, the company responsible for building the space shuttle. He was on a call in January 1986 when the shuttle *Challenger* was planning to launch in temperatures much colder than shuttle designers had ever considered safe. Seeing the amount of ice on the pad, Rocco told the folks at the Cape not to launch. NASA launched *Challenger* anyway. The crew was killed within the first two minutes.

We lost two vehicles and two crews in the end. It was too complicated of a system. We lost *Challenger* because, as I mentioned, it was too cold for a safe launch. That was a management disaster. We lost the shuttle *Columbia* because of the launch too. They shed some insulation from the external tank on ascent, and it cracked a hole in the wing. At first it seemed that nobody knew about it until the shuttle was reentering the atmosphere. That hole allowed the heat of reentry to go through that wing like a hot knife through butter. Then it turned out that NASA kind of knew there might be a problem, but they never bothered to take a look. I thought, at the time, how tragic that they never even tried to look. That was another bad management decision, but more importantly, it goes back to the basic design. I think the shuttle design was faulty.

All of the equipment we carried on our *Apollo 15* flight in 1971 was probably designed in the late 1950s. It was not new equipment—this wasn't high-tech stuff. I think that's one of the conscious decisions the rocket and spacecraft designers made. They believed we were better off with something we knew would be reliable rather than something high-tech. If it failed, there was no backup. Fortunately, the odds were high that it worked. Maybe we could have done some things a little better with newer designs, but they believed it was too risky to allow stuff that had not been proven satisfactorily. I think we were all very happy with that decision.

The space shuttle first flew in 1981, using four state-of-the-art computers, plus a fifth as a backup. It was much more complex, and at the time, it was untested. By the end of the shuttle program, those computers had become very reliable, but only because by then they had been used for so long and all the issues were understood. It's like flying a single-engine airplane compared to flying a multiengine airplane. Surprisingly, there are more accidents in multiengine airplanes than there are in single-engine craft. Why? If a single-engine airplane quits, it quits. You start looking for a place to land. Far too many people who don't have enough experience flying twin-engine airplanes lose one engine and keep on flying, maybe not realizing that airplane won't fly very well on one engine. It often happens on takeoff when instead of shutting down the other engine and crash-landing straight ahead, the pilot tries to keep going. They flip over, crash, and are killed. Simpler, and well tested, is generally better.

So why was NASA flying such a complex design? It was partially reusable, and that was going to bring the cost of going to space down so much that it would be like an airline, they said. Except, that didn't happen either.

I did some calculations. The shuttle never flew enough to get the price down very much. At the end of the shuttle program, when the shuttle costs could be fully compared to the Saturn V rocket, it turns out that they cost about the same amount per launch. Now, a Saturn V would put 260,000 pounds into Earth orbit. The shuttle, on the other hand, only ever carried one payload a little over 50,000 pounds. Why the huge difference? Because the shuttle vehicle was so damn heavy. The shuttle weighed about 165,000 pounds empty, and all of that had to be launched and come back. Unlike the Saturn V, the shuttle had to bring its heavy wings and engines back home. That only makes sense if reusing them was cheaper to do. It wasn't.

So the space shuttle could carry one-fifth of the payload, for the same amount of money, while also being a much more dangerous launch vehicle. You can understand now why I didn't want to fly it. We'd have been better off continuing to make Saturn V and Saturn IB rockets to carry payloads and crews.

The whole thing was sold to Congress and the taxpayers as a reusable system to bring costs down. I think that was absolutely a bait and switch. I believe NASA management knew what they were doing. They knew they were supposed to make low Earth orbit habitable and do a lot of work there, so they had to design a machine that could go back and forth. I think there was a psychological problem with using the Saturn V, even though it was the safest, most reliable vehicle we ever had. It was not reusable, so people assumed it would be more expensive. But the shuttle was not the right thing to do at the time, and in fact, it never was the right thing to do.

Today, with the Space Launch System rocket being built that will give us heavy-lifting capability once again, what are we making? We're remaking the Saturn V. Sure, we can call it something else if we want, and it's a little shorter and has solid rocket boosters strapped to it. But it's a Saturn V rocket in all but name. So we're going back to something that worked. But why did it take us forty years to think that through and do it? There's a real lack of planning somewhere.

That's my take on the engineering. But then there is a whole other side to it. There's the personal and the emotional side.

I never gave the shuttle much thought after my talk with Rocco. Out at NASA's Ames Research Center, I lost touch with what they were doing in Houston. By the time the shuttle finally flew, after years of delays, it had been ten years since I had flown in space. I was long retired.

After that first flight, the next five missions were all commanded by people who'd been chosen by NASA at the same time as me. Some had to wait that long for a first mission. Most had never flown to the moon. So I watched Joe Engle, Jack Lousma, Ken Mattingly, Vance Brand, and Paul Weitz command the second through sixth missions, and then they flew again along with others from my group. I was pleased for them—they were making a success of it. It looked like my astronaut selection group was making as much of an impact on the shuttle program as it had on Apollo. When Bruce McCandless, from my group, made the first untethered space walk, photos of him became as iconic as anything taken on the moon. The program wasn't living up to its wild promises—but nevertheless, what these folks were doing was really impressive.

I briefly pondered what might have happened if I had stayed at NASA. At one time, the shuttle's first flight was planned for 1978. That would still have been seven years of sitting around, testing, designing, and other office work. If I had not made a flight already, there is no question I would have stuck around. As it was, with all the shuttle delays, it would have been over ten years of waiting for a second flight. It would, however, have been my first command, so that would have been enticing.

By then, I was living in Florida, south of the Cape. To see those launches was something else. The shuttle and the Saturn V had about the same amount of thrust on launch—but the shuttle was much lighter. So it sprang off the launchpad, compared to my *Apollo 15* ride. It raced into orbit a lot faster. Because the Saturn V was so heavy and slow, you could feel the ground shake for miles when it went. That thrust was beating on the pad for a long time. The shuttle sent out a shockwave of vibration and noise, too, but it didn't last long, because it was gone so fast. Once they lit those solid rockets, like it or not, they were on their way.

In 1986 I was living down in Palm Beach, and I owned a helicopter sightseeing company in Orlando. On my way up there one morning, I stopped to get gas. As I was filling up, *Challenger* was launching. I could see the solid rockets separate, and I knew something was wrong. So I turned around, went back home, and turned on the TV—and there it was. The shuttle had torn itself apart and scattered into the ocean. No survivors. So my wife, Jill, and I didn't go to Orlando that day; we went to the Cape instead, to see the families. We were there for a couple of days, trying to be as helpful as we could. We felt that it was something we needed to do.

Some years later, we moved closer, to about sixty-five miles south of the Cape. Jill and I were right on the ocean. Because of my work at the time with the Astronaut Scholarship Foundation, we were at the Cape any time we could be, to see the launches from the closest spot anyone was allowed to view. But other times, we would stay close to home and just walk over to the beach. When those shuttles launched, we could see the whole thing—nothing was in the way of the view. I could even see shuttle launches from my backyard very clearly, going up through the trees. Sometimes the view was better from that distance, because when you got a little farther away from the Cape, you could see the arc of the shuttle as it headed out over the ocean and the whole trajectory as they headed for space.

As I watched in 2011, the very last time a shuttle launched, all my negative feelings had gone. Instead, my mood was bittersweet. It was clearly going to be the last human launch from the Cape for a long time. At that point, you forget the kind of vehicle they're flying. When you know this is the last one and we're not going to have anything even on the drawing board for many more years, you think, "Aw man. Another long gap, like there was between Apollo and the shuttle. We're really doing something wrong again." In that moment, I remembered, for all its faults, how unimaginably impressive the shuttle had been. Overall, I must admit, it was an absolutely great machine. It advanced science, made major discoveries, and built the space station. It was really a shame to retire it without having a replacement.

I headed home, poured myself a drink, looked at the ocean, and wondered when I'd next see someone launch into space from the very same pad that took me to the moon.

I'm still waiting.

(Al Worden died just seventy-three days before Americans once again launched from the Cape. When safely in orbit, the crew named their spacecraft Endeavour— *the same name Al chose for his spacecraft in 1971.)*

9

So You Want to Be an Astronaut

What do you have to do to become an astronaut? My answer to that is simple. You don't have to do anything special.

But you have to have a good education. You have to have advanced degrees. You can't just get a bachelor's degree and hope to get in. I believe it doesn't make any difference what courses you take or what curriculum you follow. I think space agencies are going to need all kinds of people in space in the future. So what's important is that you study something in school that you really love and then do really, really well at it.

If you look at those in the program today, such as the astronauts going to the International Space Station, you'll see they are a very diverse group. I think you'll find that each of them studied something in college that was their first love. They did really well at it, and as a result of that, they got into the program.

I don't think there's any magic formula. The chances of getting in are very, very slim no matter what you do. For the last NASA selection group, they had over ten thousand people apply. Yet they only pick a handful each time. So you're never guaranteed anything. I was extremely fortunate, I think, to get in. But I had all the right qualifications they were looking for back then, which are different from what they're looking for today.

Back in the Apollo program, they were looking for candidates who not only were experienced test pilots but also had academic degrees. We were in a certain age bracket and no taller than a certain height; plus we had to be in good health to pass the physical. Then we were asked to do double duty, because along with piloting the spacecraft, we also did science. Today it's much more about science—that's your way in. You don't have to be a pilot. In fact, being a pilot might not even be helpful these days.

I think that'll be the case until we start seriously thinking about going to Mars. Then I think NASA will go back to what they did before and look for people who can both fly the machine and do the science once they get there. I don't think they'll have the capacity to carry people who are only pilots or only scientists.

The International Space Station is different, because we're doing a lot of science up there, a lot of research, and so every country sends up their scientists. Helen Sharman, from England, is a good example. She's not a pilot and had no space background. But she's good at what she does, which is research chemistry. She applied and was picked out of a great mass of people, right out of thin air, to fly to a Russian space station. And I think the people we're picking in this country today for the ISS are basically scientific types who can do us some good once they get there.

So if I were a young kid today, I would be going to college and probably majoring in one of the science, technology, or math areas. I would go all the way through to get a PhD, and then I would join one of the military services and learn how to fly. Then you're double rated. You've got an academic degree, plus you've got the flight time. In twenty years, that's probably going to be what they're looking for. Plus, if you go through all of that, thinking you're going to apply to be an astronaut, but don't make it, you've still got that academic background behind you and lots of possibilities out there.

The days where only big government agencies fly in space have gone. There are all kinds of other opportunities now, whether you want to fly in space or work in the space business in general. There are companies who are promoting a ride into space, such as Virgin Galactic. They're working to take passengers on a rocket plane named SpaceShipTwo. They're going to go up and come right back down, as we used to do in F-104s and the X-15 rocket plane in the 1960s. They'll touch space, but the passengers will not really witness it for any length of time. I think that's fine if somebody wants to spend a couple of hundred thousand dollars to do that. But to me, if you're going to go into space, you have to do it in a more meaningful way. You don't just want to touch it and come right back. I don't think going straight up and straight down means much. You do get high enough that the sky turns black, and you do see what space would look like. But you only experience it for maybe a couple of minutes. And it's a very expensive thing to do. I don't see the real value in it. To me, if you're going to go into space, you've got to go into orbit. That's what I think space is all about. Even Yuri Gagarin went around the world once, and I thought that was pretty fantastic at the time.

SpaceShipTwo can't go into orbit, because it doesn't have enough energy. It goes about 2,500 miles an hour. To go into orbit, you need enough energy to get you up to 17,500 miles an hour. That's a big difference. So I think Virgin Galactic is kind of a fun thing, like an amusement ride almost, although still dangerous. You see what you want to see and go where you'd like to be, but you can't stay there.

I guess it's a first step. It's like back in the 1930s when they gave sightseeing trips in open-cockpit biplanes. They'd fly around the field once, and that was it. The passengers could technically say they'd flown. I think the suborbital stuff is similar. You can say, "Oh yeah, I've been to space. I was only there for a few minutes, but I've been there."

I ran into a guy in Ireland who'd bought a trip with XCOR and their Lynx space plane, which was a similar idea to SpaceShipTwo, although a different design. He'd paid many, many thousands of dollars for his ticket. He was an interesting guy, very enjoyable, and a great speaker with kids. Better than me, in fact. But he was out there promoting all that when Lynx was canceled. And I thought, you know, poor guy, he dumped his money into that and he's not going to make it.

I think you only get the real impact of going into space if you're there for a long enough time to really absorb what you're seeing and what it's all about. You absorb the fact that the laws of physics work, that you can go into orbit very precisely, and that you can stay at a distance away from Earth that is comfortable. If you can't spend tens of millions to go into orbit, you spend $250,000 to just take a peek, and that's it. That's all it is, just kind of a sneak peek of what it's all about up there. It seems there are a lot of people who would gladly spend that kind of money just for that. And there aren't very many people who can afford to fly faster. So far, only eight people have paid many millions to the Russians to take them into orbit. I don't blame them at all; I think it's a great thing.

Richard Garriott was one of them. He paid to go up with the Russians for twelve days to the International Space Station. He was a little kid running around my neighborhood back when I was an astronaut. His father, Owen, was an astronaut like me, and Richard grew up alongside my daughter Alison. The Garriotts lived next door to us, and those two kids used to run together in the morning back when they were both in school. Richard's a very smart guy, and he made a lot of money in programming and game design. It was wonderful to see him fly into space too.

The whole thing is so expensive that very few people are going be able to do it in the future, and so the real question is: How do we get the cost of going into space down? There are lots of ideas out there now, but we're still working with standard launch vehicles. They cost a lot of money and use a lot of fuel. We're going to have to come up with something new sometime in the future to bring that cost down so that more people can go.

I see SpaceX coming along; they've been building a Dragon spacecraft. It will allow them to fly astronauts up to the International Space Station. It's greatly needed, ever since NASA retired the space shuttle. We started flying shuttles in 1981, but right away there was a problem. When you build a shuttle, you have to ask: Where does it shuttle to? It needs to shuttle between the ground and somewhere else. At first, it didn't have anywhere to go. The shuttles were used as workhorse trucks, putting out satellites and delivering the Hubble Space Telescope. Then, finally, the International Space Station was built. At last, we had the shuttle doing meaningful transport between Earth and the station, keeping it maintained and stocked and changing over the crews. But the shuttle program was terminated in 2011. America lost the ability to get people to the station.

So we've had to fly there with the Russians, which is okay, because the Russians are extremely reliable and they do a good job. I don't have a problem with that. I just feel sad that we dropped the ball. We were the leading spacefaring nation in the world, and all of a sudden, we couldn't even get somebody up there. I think that's really a sad, sad state of affairs. We just don't have the leadership. I love Charlie Bolden, who was the NASA administrator for much of the time we have not been flying. But I think Charlie was put in a bad spot. He had a boss who was telling him what to do. And what was Charlie supposed to do—fight him? If he had, he'd have been out of a job. I think Charlie did what any reasonable person could do, and he was the best guy there at the time. He was going to work within the system to do what he could. But there were a lot of things he wasn't allowed to do.

So now we have the commercial companies such as SpaceX creating spacecraft to get there and back. Boeing is building their Starliner spacecraft. I've flown the simulator for that one up to a docking with the space station. The kids who are running that program are really impressive. Jeff Bezos has his Blue Origin spacecraft under construction, and I enjoyed checking out the prototype on their factory floor. Soon, some of these companies should be taking people up to the space station. My concern is that the only way these companies are going to get paid for doing that is by the government. So not much has changed. The government's got the money, and they used to do the job on their own. Now there are commercial companies that will do the same thing. The government is going to pay those companies, and those companies are not going to do it unless they make a profit.

So I guess I'm a little confused about why we're doing these sorts of things. There's no profit to be made except in being paid for taking somebody someplace. Perhaps a commercial company can do things less expensively than the government can because of all the bureaucracy. On the other hand, it's possible that these companies are going to be a little less concerned about things that a government agency needs to be concerned about, such as crew safety. I don't know whether we're ever going to cross a line where crew safety becomes an issue. I hope not. I hope NASA retains oversight of the absolute importance of making sure that crews are safe.

All the bureaucracy that's in government programs like the space program does not prevent people from dying. All those rules are nonsense unless the people who are in that bureaucracy are really dedicated to the safety of the crew and doing what has to be done. A very good example is the fire in the spacecraft that killed the crew of *Apollo 1* in 1967. Everybody involved in that program had a hand in making that happen. Nobody raised a red flag, saying, "There's very flammable stuff in there; we've got to be careful." Nobody raised a red flag when they decided to do a pressure check on the spacecraft using pure oxygen. Nobody raised a red flag, knowing that the hatch sealed from the inside and that if they increased the pressure in the spacecraft, the crew were not going to be able to remove that hatch. The crew, quality control, safety people, management, manufacturing—they all passed on that. And so what happened was that they got a spark in there, and in thirty seconds it was all over. Bureaucracy doesn't save you from that.

I find it difficult to believe that commercial space companies will get serious about going to Mars. What's in it for them? What are they going to find, and how are they going to get paid? Going to Mars is like doing the lunar program all over again, except ten times harder. It's going to be much longer—at least a year and a half in space. Six months going there, six months there, six months coming back. Now, if they find gold on Mars, sure, then there might be a lot of money they could make. But short of that, I don't know that they'll ever discover anything on Mars that might be valuable. Why would a guy like Elon Musk want to go to Mars? He's really dedicated to human exploration, but I think he's also a very realistic businessman. He's not going to do anything that won't at least break even. He's put a lot of his money into his space business right now, and I think he's only doing it because he envisions a return on his investment.

So in my mind, the long-distance flights we make in the future should be done by the government. But I'm not even sure a government program is capable of doing it anymore. Presently, bureaucracy is so embedded in what we do that I don't think they could ever get a program off the ground. I'm very concerned about that. We've had presidents in the past who were not big fans of the space program. It's not that they wanted to see the space program go away, but they were certainly not going to put the kind of money that it takes to go to Mars in their budgets.

NASA's budget today means that they have to do more with less. For example, look at the spacecraft that NASA's building for deep space exploration, named Orion. Now, there are people in these programs who feel differently, but this is my opinion from the outside. Why are they building Orion the way that they are? Because it looks like Apollo. It seemed easiest. All the people in Houston said, "We know how to do that, because we built Apollo." The problem is that Apollo was built decades before those guys ever got their jobs. They've had to go back to old blueprints and figure out how to do it. Nevertheless, Orion, a little bit bigger than an Apollo command module, is basically the same configuration. We've become a safety-minded bureaucracy. We will not take the big innovative leaps ahead. We will not go looking for the next paradigm in technology. Instead, we're building on something that we know something about, even though it's not really going do the job that we want it to do. It's going to be a little better than what we had before, and we can tout that. But the Orion is no better than Apollo. It's got a lift-to-drag ratio similar to the Apollo command module. So it can come back from the moon fine, at twenty-five thousand miles an hour. But if it came back from Mars directly at thirty-five thousand or forty thousand miles an hour, it wouldn't have enough lift to reenter the atmosphere easily. They'd have to skip out of the atmosphere to slow down a little and then keep doing that until they're down to a speed that they can come back in.

They are attaching Orion to a Mars transfer vehicle, to go to Mars and back, with its own propulsion system to slow down. That allows the crew to live and work somewhere very roomy on the journey. Nevertheless, I believe we need to have a much more capable spacecraft than Orion. As a matter of fact, I even went to NASA Headquarters and tried to pitch a different entry vehicle. They asked me to do that, but only after Houston had established their design criteria for Orion. So there was no way I could get a capable spacecraft into the mix. It is therefore a nonsymmetric spacecraft, because to get the lift, you've got to provide some nonsymmetric air flows. I think that's a shame. We should have had the courage, conviction, and foresight to say, "Okay, we're going to take a technological leap here, do something new, and build a big leap forward."

I think the Chinese are going to have humans on Mars long before we do. I think they're very capable. They've been sending people to their own space station. Why do they have their own? Because we won't work with them. What kind of nonsense is that? I mean, we're space-trained nations; why aren't we working with the Chinese? Because we've got some gripe—we don't like their politics. I was invited to go check out their space facilities the other year, but the State Department wouldn't allow it, which I thought was dumb. And why are they so capable in space? Basically, because we trained them all. I was asked to present a scholarship at a university in Michigan a few years ago, in a big auditorium full of students. In the question-and-answer period after the scholarship presentation, somebody asked, "Are we going to go back to the moon?"

I replied, "Oh, no question about it—somebody will go to the moon."

"Who?"

"The Chinese. They're getting ready to go now. They're very good. They'll go."

The back two rows of the auditorium stood up and started cheering. They were all Chinese. We are training their students to compete with us, which in my opinion seems like a really dumb thing to do. Last I checked, China graduates ten times more engineers than America. They're going to do some very impressive things. They have a much more structured government, and right now they want to go into space to prove to the whole world that they can. Apollo happened not only because the American government set the goal but because it made sure the money was there. When you've got those things going for you, the bureaucracy disappears, and everybody looks to the goal. I'm sure that's the way the Chinese look at it. They're probably going to land people on Mars way, way before us.

In the meantime, I wish you luck trying to get into space. Perhaps you'll pay the thousands for that suborbital hop. Perhaps the millions for a week or two on the space station. The ultimate way, of course, is to do what I did— get somebody else to pay for your trip. I have no definitive idea of what it cost the government, but I've heard *Apollo 15* cost $500 million. So if you break that up three ways, it cost over $165 million to send me to the moon and back.

Did they get their money's worth out of me? I don't know. I'd like to think so, but somebody else might disagree. Personally, I think exploring the moon was priceless.

10

Thoughts after a Moon Voyage

I'm better at flying jets than writing poems. Nevertheless, I started writing them when I was an astronaut.

When I came back from the moon, my friends and neighbors threw a party. And then another. And another. Every night. In my own apartment. I was working all day, doing extensive debriefings about our mission with all the NASA folks. I would come home physically drained, only to find a party in full swing. Pretty soon they were going late into the night, and I finally had to say, "Okay, everybody, I've got to go to sleep." They just wanted to be around somebody who had returned from the moon.

So they all left. But then, I couldn't sleep.

I would sit in my living room, turn all the lights out, and . . . nothing. I was just overly exhausted at that point. I'd finally get five hours of sleep at most, get up, and drag myself through the debriefings again for another day. This went on for a couple of weeks.

That's where the poetry started coming from.

It would be quiet at one o'clock in the morning, but my head was still going a mile a minute. So I grabbed some old coffee-stained legal pads and started writing, and that's what came out. It kind of flowed freely. I wasn't really thinking about it; I'd simply sit there in the dark and write this stuff down. I was discussing the hard engineering facts during the day, and then at night I was sitting there thinking about all this other stuff and putting it on paper. I looked at it later and thought, "Oh, if I just tweaked this a little bit, why, it would be okay." It was my own personal debriefing after going to the moon.

So I did a bunch of them. There were some people in a poetry group in Houston I talked to, and they were enthused about what I was doing. They said I should really publish them. But I kind of let it sit off to the side and didn't really do anything with it. Until one day, I was talking to Fred Rogers, and I sent some of it up to him. He liked it and got in touch with one of the editors at *Family Circle*. Fred then invited me up to New York to talk about a book—and the next thing I knew, they were publishing it. The poetry book was named *Hello Earth: Greetings from Endeavour*.

I am not much into writing poetry today, though I feel the urge now and then. I hadn't read my poems for some time, but I went to reread all of them recently to see if there were any old memories hidden in there. I found those old legal pads, including some poems never published back then and alternate versions of ones that were. I hope you enjoy this different way of experiencing space with me. You could think of them either as poems or as the free-flowing words of someone still absorbing the experience of spaceflight.

RISING FROM EARTH

A vibration, a roar
Motion
Shaking, rattling we lift
Straight up

We climb on plumes of thunder
Into a rising sun
And away from reality

Goodbye my friends
You are gone
The whole world has gone
On a trip

But this must be finished
Faster, faster, can't turn back
Insignificant, I am insignificant

Lights flash, panel moves
Floating in nothingness
Then softly, softly
The movement begins again
Push up the switch
And suddenly light everywhere

Earth is floating aimlessly, serenely
Peopled, I know, by intelligent life
Man is ever driven on
Vision greater than deed

Floating so far
Extending the realm of man
Born again in light of day
And everything is suddenly right

ALTERNATE VERSION OF "OCEANS"

The ocean forms a solid line
Where water meets the sky
I sense that I could touch it
If I could only fly

Pelicans glide in a single file
Waves try to climb up the beach
But die in the attempt
While fins show the presence of sharks below
Taunting in their contempt

At night I hear the waves roll in
While watching the stars roll out
They seem to beckon me and say
You're the only one about

I'd say I'd like to join you
In your infinite ocean of play
But how can I leave the loveliness
I've witnessed here today?

So if you will allow me
I'll meet you half the way
At a place between us called the moon
Where I can briefly stay

My bird is over behind the dunes
Like a comet I can drive
Out to the moon to meet you
The mighty Saturn Five

ALTERNATE VERSION OF "LAUNCH FROM THE BLEACHERS"

The hour draws near
For the ceremony to commence
The tiny van draws close
And the three enter her belly
She calms, but for a moment
The time is near

The incision in her head is closed with force
Her mind starts to function
As white room falls away
And the van returns
From whence it came

Not yet!
And now the clock rolls on
To mark a time in history
Almost there
A hush falls on the crowd

She is about to fly
And leave her lover
Standing on the pad
I long to be with her

The sun is high today
The sky is clear
Goodbye my love
I seem to hear

The fire is under her now
The crowds begin to cheer
And some cry

And suddenly she moves
The child is being born
Of Earth and heaven
And all the stars

She's born
Hearts leap in those who watch
And tears of pride flow free
The purest of our minds and souls
Have witnessed history

ALTERNATE VERSION OF "PERSPECTIVE"

Within the confines of a mechanical marvel
Stars whirl around, pirouette for us to see and wonder
How vast is this universe?
Where is the order?
We must be a part of the pattern.

Some put it in simple, youthful terms
To learn of ourselves, we must study others
To search for clues to our history
But what is to be gained?
What is the purpose?

And then, breathtaking view
The earth drifts majestically into sight.

And suddenly the purpose is clear
Because we are not trying for a closer look
At our faithful companion the moon
We are sent far away to look back
At our home, the earth.

To realize how beautiful, how precious, and how fragile
The view cannot be duplicated
From any vantage point anchored
In the rocks of old.

I must return
They have followed the wrong path
With help it can be corrected
We must go on.

ALTERNATE VERSION OF "MOONSCAPE"

Quietly, silently, floating, flying
Smoothly, fluidly, turning, gliding
Pumps hum, fans whirr
Radios buzz, computers purr

Each crater is different, together they ring
Of history past, seen in the present
Dreamlike, creamlike, this orbiting crescent

If there were time, they would tell a lot
Of forming the moon, when the sun was hot
Where empty nights meet blazing days
Crushed legacy of ancient skin

ALTERNATE VERSION OF "APOLLO LOST"

Say to me you cannot do it
Say to me, do not explore
Then I will do it, to wit
Today if not before

THE DEATH

Apollo died tonight
Of alcohol poison it's said
But in the eyes of those present
It died of self-importance and pity.

The wake was a dinner
At the Yacht Club of course
And the Father said a prayer
But Apollo won't be back.

We all feasted on the body Apollo
And lived by the rules he set
Apart from society
A part of society.

Who killed the great god Apollo?
Is a question of importance
Who will keep the legions of Apollo alive?
Is a question of crucial importance.

ALTERNATE VERSION OF "TRAINING"

Rendezvous and docking
Held steady and sure
We'll never get home
With the problems to cure.

Machines and things
Until the head stings
I'll never get it
My mind seems to say.

But what I missed last week
I'll get right today
It goes on and on
Then it suddenly pays.

UNTITLED

We are
What we are
We are
All!
In the timeless universe
Of the great crab spiraling outward
Or the black hole spiraling inward
We look about
And watch the hooded men do their magic
And fix infinity

At the right instant
A gull flies slowly across the setting sun
Far out to sea—alone
I am that bird
We are that bird
The fawns stop beside a quiet road
And join us in solitude
The hawk slowly wheels
Like a great constellation
Telling fortunes
Trees crash over in a primordial forest
And today we hear the sound
In exhausts and smoke stacks
The beginning is the end
In ever-increasing circles

UNTITLED

What do you think of the face of the moon?
Doesn't it look sad?
If you could see the other side
You'd say, "It does look glad!"
Because it doesn't have to look
At Earth and you and me
And witness all the wars we've wrought
To prove our destiny.

Maybe she's our guardian
To see us through our trials
To wait with grace
In her lonely place
Until we have space
For every race
And fought our fights and won our wars
Returning ever more to those peaceful shores
For whence we came on primal Earth
When she was midwife at our birth.

UNTITLED

Voices calling in my mind
Urging a return to the center
Of all life and existence
Return to the eternal mentor
To meet those who have preceded
An earthly form
Oh, Zeus, where are you now?
I hear your call in the night
They say you touched lightly
On an Earth troubled with doubt
And spawned a race of gods
But where did you go?

11

Risk and Death

As a pilot and astronaut, how I think about death is quite different from many others. I believe it's hard to decide how to live unless you know how much you are willing to risk.

When I lay at the top of the Saturn V rocket on launch morning for a mission to the moon, I knew there was a risk. In an intellectual way, I understood and accepted the dangers. If I hadn't, I would not have been there. I believed that the probability of failure of any lunar flight was about 10 percent. So, one out of ten—I took my chances. And that's not all I had to weigh that morning.

I had to understand what else was at stake. My decision was very different from a pilot flying in combat, for example, because in combat the TV cameras are not on you. There are not a million people watching you. On a lunar flight, there's more at risk than just getting there and coming back. It's doing the job correctly so that everybody can see what you've done. There's national prestige on your shoulders.

I've heard that when World War II started, British fighter pilots knew that their chance of survival was 10 percent. As the war progressed, those odds improved, because they shot down more and more German airplanes. But at first, many who flew from England to Germany believed they probably had a 50 percent chance of surviving a single bombing run. And guess what—they still took the risk. Huge numbers of them didn't come back. I think there's always that personal decision to make in an endeavor that involves risk. What I did, by comparison, was much safer. No one was actively trying to kill me.

So just like those pilots did in World War II, I rationalized how important it was to my country that I did this right. It's not just getting to the moon and back. You understand that history is going to remember you forever, even if it doesn't work out. If worse came to worst and we perished on the flight,

I could rationalize in my mind that I had done my best and just hope that it wasn't me who caused the accident that took us out.

People ask me, "Weren't you nervous on launch?" And because of that philosophy—and I don't go into that with a lot of people, but because of that—I have to tell them, "No, I was not." We were either going make it or not. Why get excited about it? Getting excited was not going to change our chances one bit, so you might just as well calm down, do your job, and stay cool. If we had perished on launch, so what? We would have accepted that. We accepted that before we took the flight.

I adopted kind of a Japanese philosophy about that, where there's something more important than you. Your life is unimportant compared to whatever you're doing that is important for your country. That is why Japan had kamikaze pilots in World War II. What they had to do for their country was more important than their own lives. Personally, I could never go that far. I think knowingly flying off to die is very different from taking the risk that it might happen.

When I was a student at the University of Michigan, living on campus, I had a Japanese friend. He was an older man—older than I was anyway, probably in his midtwenties—and a fellow engineering student. I would meet him just about every day at the drugstore to have a cup of coffee and a doughnut before I went to class. After a while, he began to tell me of his life in the Japanese military. He'd been selected as a kamikaze pilot late in the war. That blew my mind. He was prepared to do his duty, totally dedicated to his country. He would've done it—he actually would have flown an airplane into a ship. He was scheduled for a mission the day the war ended, so he was saved. I don't know how or why he decided to complete his college education in the States, but he came to Michigan in about 1950 to finish an engineering degree. He was a nice little guy, very friendly, and not hung up on the war at all.

I always thought that it's just so hard to believe that somebody would do that. But that comes back to the point I am making about there being something bigger than you as an individual. That's what that kamikaze thing was all about. The country was so important that his attitude was, "My life is unimportant compared to what I can do for the country." Then he ended up in America, ten years later, studying with the people he was ready to kill.

Joe Kittinger, the aviation trailblazer who almost died during the Vietnam War, said it best: "Fighter pilots and test pilots do not accept death. They accept the risk of death." I totally agree with what Joe was saying. The mark of a test pilot is that when his airplane is spiraling into the ground and in twenty seconds he's going to die, he is still calmly reading off all the stuff on his instrument panel to the folks on the ground. You allow that if that risk comes to you, if it becomes a reality, you'll accept it. You do your job as best you can, which is to tell everybody on the ground what's happening and why. When the end comes, it comes. That's the way it is.

I was reminded of that in 1969 when the *Apollo 12* mission launched. They got off the launchpad in bad weather. Lightning struck the spacecraft. They lost their main power supply. What did Pete Conrad, the commander, do? He laughed. He read off everything he could to the ground: "We've lost this. We've lost that." Now, that thing could've blown up. That crew didn't know if they were going to make it or not. But Pete just kept reading off stuff the way he was supposed to, while they fixed the problem. He was a true test pilot. That's the way you do things.

Pam, my wife at the time I joined NASA, was very sensitive to these kinds of things. It wasn't just that I was taking the risk of flying to the moon. She and I had been together since I was at West Point, and she knew there was a risk that any husband who was in the military might die. The problem was that I was taking bigger and bigger risks. Going to pilot training was one thing. Going to test pilot school was another. Joining the space program was getting to the end of the road for her. Imposed on top of this, every camera in the world was stuck in her face whenever she went outside the house. The news people followed her around all the time. NASA wanted her to tell the press, "Oh, I'm fine with it. I'm proud, happy, and thrilled." She wasn't. She was scared to death.

The strange part to me at the time was that her way out was to get divorced. Well, okay, I thought at the time, so you get divorced. Now it doesn't make any difference whether I live or die. If you had stayed and took the gamble with me and I survived it all, guess what? We'd be fine. But based on the gamble that I might die during the flight, she disappeared from my life. I was so wrapped up in what I was doing at the time that it took me decades to understand that it was too much for her. It's too late for me to say sorry. And I wasn't about to turn down a flight to the moon.

Pam had what I considered an ahimsa philosophy to life—that is, a deep respect for all living things and an avoidance of harm to anyone. She wouldn't even step on a spider. It's something you find within the beliefs of Buddhism and Jainism. Life is sacred, and every other soul must be protected. In contrast, I was doing something very counterintuitive to human nature—I was choosing to put my life in danger. For me, if I died, I would be gone, and I wouldn't care. She, on the other hand, would have been left with the feeling of a spouse lost forever. If she and I were divorced first, she reasoned, she could have already established her own life and would be separated from my demise. It's one way of insulating yourself from death.

Death has a way of finding you at different times in your life. The first time I truly recall witnessing death was during my first assignment as a fighter pilot. I was on alert, ready to take off at any moment. The alert ground crew was driving a tug across the runway back to the hangar just as a C-47 transport airplane was landing. I don't know how they got their signals mixed up, but the ground crew proceeded as if the runway was clear. The C-47 hit them broadside and killed the three airmen in the tug. The wheels of the C-47 went right through the cab of the tow truck. I was on the scene at the runway within minutes, but there was nothing anyone could do.

Another incident occurred a few years later, in England, when I was at the Empire Test Pilot School. A very accomplished and highly respected French aviator named François was making a test flight, and on the way back to Farnborough, he hit a hill. The hill was covered with fog, and I don't think he ever saw it. They got his remains back that night, and the next morning at about six thirty, we all formed up close to the flight line, wearing black armbands. We slow marched his casket to the airplane that would take him home. It was a very emotional time, but the Brits were very stiff-lipped. And we all followed suit. It was an incredibly somber event.

The surreal thing about this was that the U.S. Navy Test Pilot School was visiting at the same time, and we'd had to wine and dine them the night he crashed. I don't think any of us went home that night after the party but instead went directly to the flight line to see François off. The navy guys were never aware of the tragedy. As soon as the plane took off, we went back to looking after them.

I remember watching the guys doing this, and I thought that the British were really amazing. They paid him the highest respect they could, and then they turned right around and entertained the Navy Test Pilot School. They were flexible enough to do that. I thought that was marvelous. It's no wonder I learned to do the same.

I'd also attended West Point, where we lived by the Cadet Honor Code, and this related very much to my feelings on launch day. What is more important than your own life? It's the honor of doing what you have to do. Honor—my honor—was more important than whether I lived or died on that flight. And my only thought was, "If we die on this flight, I hope it was not caused by something I did." That's the big thing. I think any test pilot has the same thought process. You go through a long, long training period to become a test pilot, and it's not all about flying airplanes. It's about how you conduct yourself when you're flying flight-test airplanes. It has to do with accepting death as a natural result of what you are doing. I always thought it was interesting that when we had the fire at the Cape in 1967 that killed the crew of *Apollo 1*, I know of at least three test pilots who died that same week flying new airplanes. Where did they show up in the papers? *Apollo 1* was page 1, with pictures and everything. The three test pilots' deaths were on page 19. The pervasive philosophy in the test pilot group was that we had to dedicate our lives to helping develop the best airplanes in the world. And we were willing to die for it, because that was what our country needed. I don't want to be holier-than-thou about anything, but there is something about honor and doing the right thing for your country. I felt it very strongly during my spaceflight.

So I was prepared to die in space. There is another thought I had about that. If mission control knew of a huge, potentially fatal issue, should they have told us?

I remember how John Glenn, flying America's first orbital space mission, was not told about a potential issue with his heat shield. He raised hell about that when he got back, and he was right to do so. The flight controllers should have told him. It was the same on our flight, where Jim Irwin was having heart irregularities on the way back from the moon, but they never told our commander and let Jim do a partial EVA. That put us in danger.

But what if I'd been the commander of the *Columbia* space shuttle on its final mission? What if mission control had correctly worked out that the damage the shuttle sustained on launch meant it could never return?

I have mixed feelings. If I were that commander, I would want to know what was going on. But from the point of view of the public and mission control, should they have told the crew they were going to die in a week? I mean, who wants to do that? What benefit would there be in telling them? I think I would want to know, if for no other reason than to work out how to create the most painless death for my crew.

So death has never been an abstract, philosophical thing for me in my career. It has been real, when fellow pilots crashed and astronauts whom I knew died doing their jobs. But it was never as real for me as when I lost Jill. When I lost my wife.

In 2012, thirty years after we got married, Jill noticed an unnatural swelling in her stomach. She went to the doctor, who told her it was nothing to worry about. But it continued to bother her. That summer, she went to a different doctor, who did a lot of poking and prodding but still couldn't see any problem.

By Christmas, she was really beginning to feel badly. I knew that something was seriously wrong with her. So on New Year's Eve, I pleaded with her to go to her personal physician in Florida and not leave until she could find out what the problem was. She did, and after a lot of discussion, her doctor sent her over to have a CT scan.

Then that doctor called me and said, "Come on over to the office." So I went over, and Jill and I sat there. When the doctor came in, she had the report on the CT scan with her, and she was visibly upset. I knew something really bad was going on. Finally, she took Jill's hands, held them, looked at her, and said, "Jill, you've got cancer."

It was the worst news that anybody could hear. The doctor went on: "We do not know how far advanced it is. We're going to run some tests, and we think that you also need to go to a cancer center and be evaluated."

I knew there were two places I could take her. We had no faith in the local hospitals. So I made an appointment for her at a highly regarded cancer center in Tampa. They did another test on her, and what came back from that test was that she had the highest cancer numbers they'd ever seen—unbelievably high. Her doctor there was just blown away by the high number. So they scheduled her for surgery a week later, and she went under the knife.

The cancer had attached itself in a couple of places, and when she came home after the surgery, life was very different. I went through a large learning curve of how to care for her. I was making constant runs to the medical supply store, and we kind of fumbled our way through how to live. Every Monday morning, I would drive her to chemotherapy for two or three hours. When I drove her back home, she was okay that day, but the next day, she was really out of it. She was really, really not good. It would take two or three days for her to kind of work her way back out of that.

From the time I brought her back home, I never left her side. Never. I was so impressed with how Jill handled it all. She never complained. When we would go out to do the chemo, she always took something for the nurses, such as a box of cookies. They got to expecting it and were glad to see her coming, because she was so generous with other people.

We would leave the cancer center and almost invariably stop at a McDonald's, where she would have a little dish of ice cream. That was about the only thing she could keep down. We did this for probably twenty-two weeks beginning in the summer of 2013.

It was a totally different, new world for both of us. I was with her all the time for the next two years. I quit the work I had been doing. There were a couple of rare exceptions when she was doing fine and it was okay for me to briefly leave. But otherwise, no one else saw much of me. Yet those last years were unbelievable for me. How good she was. How strong, courageous, friendly, and generous.

Her cancer numbers came down. In early 2014 she was even able to have another internal operation to make daily life easier for her. The doctors were so happy with her, clapping and jumping around and having a party. I brought her back home. She seemed back to normal.

It wasn't more than a month later that she started throwing up after every meal.

We couldn't figure that out. So I took her back up to the doctors, who opened her up again and took a look. Twenty-five minutes later Jill was back, all sewn up, and the doctor told me, "I'm sorry, the cancer has spread, and it's all through her stomach and other organs too. There's nothing we can do."

I asked, "Well, how long do we have?" The doctor replied, "Well, you might have up to six months." I planned on taking her up to a lake house in Michigan we had bought but never lived in. She had only ever visited it for ten days. It was a beautiful, peaceful place far away from daily troubles. "Yeah," they said, "that would be a good idea if you could do that."

First, she'd have to be well enough to travel. I arranged for the ambulance to take her directly to a hospice in Florida. She got a lovely room with a nice screened porch. She was happy there. The staff was wonderful to her there. But part of the reason they were so good was that she was so good. She always smiled and had a big welcome for everybody.

Medical insurance would only pay for five days there. But it was clear she was happiest there, so I said, "I'll just pay. Whatever it takes."

Because she could not process food, they had to insert a tube through her stomach wall. From then on, as often as I could, I'd feed her a milkshake, and then half an hour later I would open up that peg tube and try to drain out as much as I could. That was the only kind of nourishment she could handle, and it was a terrible way to try to absorb nutrients. But there wasn't anything else we could do. Her condition did not improve. The Michigan plan fell away.

Her family came in—cousins, children, friends from all over the country. We knew it was only a matter of time. She was so gracious and so happy to see everybody. Her personality had always been one of a meeter and greeter. She made everyone feel comfortable. But it was really sad, because, basically, everybody was saying goodbye.

They had a room I could stay in there. Our daughter Tammy was staying as well. And one morning, around five, they came and got us both and told us, "She's gone."

Instead of six months, it had only been six weeks.

The morning she died, she looked good. She really looked good. I don't think the cancer had got her as much as her heart just quit. She avoided some terrible, terrible times that would have been ahead with that cancer.

Jill and I had our ups and downs throughout our three decades of marriage. She'd always had an Irish temper, and that came to the surface a lot of times during our marriage. We fought about a lot of things. But like any relationship, we worked our way through those issues.

When she got sick, that all went away. There were no issues at all anymore. I think the fact that I was with her all the time made a big difference for her. I did not ignore her. I did not leave her. I did not turn away from her. I was there, all the time. When she had any medical setbacks, I'd clean her up, get her back in bed, comfort her, and spend hours just talking. I think that's the kind of thing that brought us even closer together.

And then she was gone.

I was very depressed. I can't even tell you. For a while, I just kind of hung on. I went back to Michigan that summer, out to the lake house, where I had planned to take Jill. I became a hermit. I would sit there all day long, in a chair, just looking out at the lake.

When you lose somebody like that and you're living by yourself, it gets to be pretty lonely.

Thank goodness for my neighbors. They wouldn't let me sit there too long, without strolling over and saying, "Come over and have a drink." They were good friends, and they were good to me. They gradually got me out of it, and we went and played golf a few times.

I spent the summers of 2014 and 2015 there at the lake. In the meantime, I did all the stuff that I needed to do to get the house completed. But when I went up in the summer of 2016, I realized I had to get out of there. It wasn't so much about Jill—she'd only ever been there for ten days. But that lake is thirty-five miles out of town, thirty-five miles to the nearest hospital, and I was there by myself. I just said to myself, "Hey, you know, this is stupid. You've got a phone, yeah, sure, but what good's that going to do you?"

So I decided to sell it.

I also decided that the best therapy for me was to be busy. Fortuitously, back in early 2015, I'd had a message from Jason Rubin, a good buddy who works in the international air show business. He said, "Would you like to come to the Paris Air Show and work with us in the U.S. Pavilion?" And I replied, "You know, that would probably be a good thing for me to do."

So I really keep myself busy. There are always things going on. If I am going overseas, I try to book a bunch of other events while I am over there, to make all that travel worth it. If I'm going to Europe, I tell everybody and let them know what my schedule is, and if they want to tag something on before or after, fine. That's why I am sometimes away almost a whole month. Staying busy has been the key for me.

When I pass on, I just want people to say I was a good man. In the meantime, I have good friends and a lot of work. It keeps me young and moving. I'm getting to the point now where I don't need to do quite so much. I'll probably try to just do the bigger events and let the little ones go by the wayside.

I still think like a pilot—that is, I don't think too much about death. I spend time thinking about lost colleagues. But that's because, having all survived flying to the moon, everyone's now in their eighties and nineties, and the inevitable is happening.

It was always interesting to me that Tom Wolfe's big thing was talking about death and how test pilots accept death. That's what his whole book *The Right Stuff* was about, really. But when it gets to this point in life, losing a colleague is a different thing altogether.

I have to laugh, in fact, when I'm out giving talks in public and a guy or a girl comes up to me and says, "Oh, I remember your flight! I was five years old, and I watched the launch!" I look them dead in the eye, and I say, "Thanks for reminding me how old I am!"

I tend not to go to funerals. I would go to a funeral to celebrate the person who died. But they don't know that—they're dead! So why do we go to funerals? Well, it's because of all the other people who are going. And in many of those cases, I don't know those people. So am I going to go to a funeral to help them? Probably not. It's just not something that I would want to do. I worry about those instead who are still alive, some of whom are dear friends, and are not in the best of health.

One funeral I was determined to be at, however, was that of my fellow astronaut and great friend Dick Gordon, who died in 2017. It was not easy for me to get there, but I was asked by the family if I'd talk at his memorial, which I was delighted to do, because I owe everything to Dick. I thought it was appropriate, but I did not want to say anything heavy. I looked at it more as a celebration of Dick's life than a funeral service. And I think that's the way Dick would have wanted it to be too.

It's different for the public. In terms of symbolism, a chapter will close when the last moon voyager goes. That'll be the end of it. And then it'll just be pure history. Before that, there will be one last person alive who went to the moon. There are guys younger than me who have been there, so it probably won't be me. It's going to be a big deal for the media. Especially the last moonwalker. It will be quite a legacy, and I wonder how that guy will deal with it. It will be interesting.

When Dick Gordon's beloved wife, Linda, died, Dick and I had a long talk. I was saying how sorry I was, what a great girl she was, and that I knew how hard it would be for him. Dick cut right through me and said, "No, no, don't talk like that. We had a wonderful life. She lived a really good, full life. And you don't need to feel sorry about it at all."

It's true. We have had good, long lives. We made it. And when I think of bravery and heroes and courage in the face of death, I no longer think of other pilots.

I think of Jill.

12

The Point of the Space Program

So what's the point of all of this?

For decades, people have asked me: Why are we journeying into space? Especially when we have so many problems to fix right here on Earth?

There are many good answers to that. What I can do—perhaps all I can do—is share my personal experience.

There's a place on the other side of the moon that is very special to me. You'll already know of the dark side of the moon, which is the side facing away from the sun. Then there's the back side of the moon, which is the side away from Earth. They are not always the same, but they frequently overlap while the moon orbits Earth. When I was out there, orbiting for three days on my own, there was about a quarter section of my trajectory around the moon that was in the shadow of both the sun and Earth. You can't see it from Earth. You have to be there.

During my training, we had selected thirty-seven of the brightest stars to use as navigational aids. A lot of my training involved learning how to find those stars, based on guide stars that would lead me to them. There were certain patterns I knew to look for. But when I got into that quarter section behind the moon, I lost all that.

"Oh my god," I thought, "I can't believe there are so many stars out there."

I've heard that under the best seeing conditions on Earth, people with great eyesight can make out over nine thousand individual stars. On Earth the atmosphere diminishes the fainter stars to the point that when we look at the sky at night, we don't see all the little dim stars out there. The atmosphere really absorbs a lot of the light. When I was in that special part of my lunar orbit, I could see so many more than that. The sheer volume washed out the individual starlight in the sky—all I could see was a blur of light. It was unbelievable. I could make out some of the brighter navigational stars shining through, but they were hard to pick out individually. I understood—in a way that I had never felt before, because I was actually seeing it myself—that I was looking through the galaxy we live in. The galaxy that we are part of. It's a huge difference to mentally take in and try to wrap your mind around.

There are hundreds of billions of stars in our galaxy. Knowing that number from my training took away any uncertainty about what I was looking at. When you put that many stars out in front of you, they're going to wash each other out. I was seeing the whole thing. I could see the mountaintops of the moon on the horizon, not because they were lit, but because of the light they cut off. The stars were so thick that they made a clear, distinct horizon of the mountains. That was just absolutely mind-blowing to me.

The Hubble Space Telescope is beginning to bring to our attention a lot of things we never realized or thought of before. But when we see the stunning images it returns, we're looking at pictures. They're amazing, they're unbelievable, but they're just pictures. It's so very different with the naked eye.

There's a record I set out there that often gets overblown. While on the far side of the moon, I was farther away from any other human being than anyone else had been before or has since. There were two people on the other side of that rock, and everybody else was a quarter of a million miles away back on Earth. With the moon's bulk in the way, I couldn't talk to anyone else by radio either. I was totally alone. While this wasn't really a big deal to me, my guess is that my personal experience was amplified by that solitude and personal reflection.

I think about the personalities of the other two guys I was with for the rest of that mission. Dave Scott was very scientific, straightforward, and mathematical. Jim Irwin was religious. I doubt I would have had the thoughts I had if those guys were with me at the time. They would have been saying other things, trying to bring me back down to reality. But all by myself, I could let my mind just open up and see all of it.

We can sit on Earth and read about this—at least, I assume that's where you're reading this book. But think of it this way: You can research visiting a foreign country as much as you like. Yet until you go, until you've had that experience in person, you can't truly know it or feel it. Being out there expanded my understanding of who we are and where we are.

I was so blown away by what I could see that I began to realize, hey, we're not really looking at all of this in the right way. We have a hard time opening up our minds to things that we don't know or understand. We need to expand our view. I think this is a failing we humans have. We are so quick to develop theories about things we can see, touch, measure, and weigh. We don't have a really good ability to think beyond that. I mean, a scientist wants data. And that data is going to prove certain things. But beyond that, there's often not a lot of conjecture. I don't see people extending what they know into regions they don't know, because we don't have the ability to do that, really. So all the things we think about the universe are based on what we can see and measure. I think there's so much more to it out there than that, and we just haven't seen it yet. We are just not advanced enough to really understand all of that.

After a couple of days in space, I had also become very comfortable without the effects of gravity. In fact, I got so comfortable that I began to think, "You know what? Genetically, we understand spaceflight. We have something in our minds that makes us very comfortable in space." Some liken it to being a fetus in the womb, but I don't know about that. I think that we have a genetic memory, like going back to something we're familiar with.

When you ask an astronomer how many galaxies there are in the universe, they'll tell you about two trillion. And if you ask them how many universes they think there are, most will tell you, "We don't know. There might be more than one." Just a few decades ago they would have thought you were crazy to even ask that last question. I think the universe is very logical, but we tend to think of it in a different way. I would suspect that there are big bangs going on all the time, creating new universes, and it's a never-ending process.

This is what I began to ponder as I looked out there, through those hundreds of billions of stars. I understood as never before that the chances of there being a planet that could sustain life is a positive number. I don't care what the number is—it could be a one hundredth of a percent. But there has to be another planet out there that can sustain life. And if a planet can sustain life, it's probably going to have life. The chances of that life being older than us is a virtual certainty, because we are a very young, intelligent species in terms of universal time. We think of our culture in terms of thousands of years. Our universe has had billions of years for things to develop.

Gazing deep into our universe, I felt that there must be other intelligent life out there. I began to appreciate efforts to search for it a lot more, because I think the time will come when we will probably get some kind of signal. That's not to say I believe in aliens flying UFOs, because I don't. I think UFOs are figments of people's imaginations or photographs they doctored or something commonplace that can't be easily recognized. If there are actually UFOs, bring me a piece of one that I can analyze and confirm that it's not something from Earth.

But getting back to my main point, I began to realize that we are not a species who is serious about a plan to survive. I started to feel, and I still believe, that the real reason for the space program is to give humanity the capability to go somewhere else. I began to read books on the subject, including the symbiotic relationship between humans and machines. I've concluded that the imperative of all living creatures on Earth is for the species to survive. It could be grass, it could be trees, animals—anything. The imperative is to survive. Everything that is alive has a mechanism for casting its seed so that even if the original organism dies, it has seeds out there that are going survive and be okay. One of the examples that fascinated me was the indigenous people of the Polynesian islands in the Pacific Ocean. They all probably came from the same place originally, but perhaps a volcano erupted, so they got into canoes and went to the next island. Then something else happened, maybe a natural disaster or a war. They got in their canoes once again, and they went to the next place. Pretty soon, they've radiated out to occupy all the islands in the Pacific. Instead of one group living in one place that could be wiped out, now you've got a thousand different groups out there, and if any one of them gets knocked out, the rest are okay.

I think that is the nature of all living things. It's in their nature to survive, and I think we're no different. So I have developed this idea that genetically we're driven to space, not just to explore, but in a way that, over time, with technological development, we'll go wherever we want. We're actually going to be able to do what we see in *Star Trek*. The big impediment right now is speed; we don't have a propulsion system that can help us right now. We're pretty much limited to chemical stuff. We'll have to solve the problem of the speed of light. To me, that obstacle is just that—an obstacle. A hundred years ago we were at the same point with the speed of sound. In 1947 we found out that, yeah, we can fly through it. Today, every single military fighter I know of is a supersonic fighter, and there's nothing to it.

I am convinced that someday some bright mathematician is going to figure out how to solve some equations regarding the theory of relativity. I think someday we're going to take these problems beyond speculative theories. Whether it is a thousand years, or ten thousand, or a hundred thousand years from now, we'll have it solved. We'll be able to go to other Earth-like planets. We know of some promising candidate planets as close as four light-years away—as near as it gets in our galactic neighborhood.

I traveled the farthest that humanity has ever been, where I could block the light of Earth with my outstretched thumb. And yet I know it was a baby step. We got to the moon with the technology that we developed. The next step is going to require more technology, but it's just another step. Mars is next. We might then go to one of the moons of Jupiter. As a country, right now, I believe we're trying to build a strategy that says what the steps are going to be.

So that's what I think the space program's all about. We are really infants in developing a capability to protect ourselves. The truth is that we're not always going to be able to live here on Earth. We know that. That time might be five billion years in the future, when our sun dies, but there's no time like now to get started. I keep going back to the old Chinese axiom that says, "A journey of a thousand miles starts with a single step." And we've made that one small step, going to the moon. The next step out will be Mars. I've got nothing against going to Mars. I mean, okay, it's nice to go there. I think Mars is something people relate to in terms of us going and finding out what's there. I think there's at least some small possibility that we might find something on Mars that would make it more friendly toward us than what we see right now. They're finding stuff such as possible evidence of water there. It's going to be another paradigm shift in how we approach things and how we develop technology to do that program.

What the planet Mars really does is give us the incentive to develop the technology to get there. The farther out we go, the more technology we're going to have to develop. Eventually we're going to have to cross the barrier where we develop a propulsion system that's going to get us almost anywhere we want. And I think that will happen someday, because we are an assertive, intelligent species. We're not going to let obstacles get in our way forever, even though they seem insurmountable at present.

There are a lot of dangers in humans traveling to Mars. For one thing, we're physically not equipped to do long-term stuff without fixing ourselves in some way. We'll solve those problems. I believe that when we develop the capability to go as quickly as we want somewhere, the whole issue will go away. Until then, we'll have to build machines big enough to install centrifuges. In many science fiction movies, there's a mechanism somewhere in which they can exercise in a proper way in a one-g environment. I think they've got it right, with a ring that rotates, giving them their exercise capability. These kinds of problems we can solve; I see no issue there. But I already believe we're genetically okay to go into space, because we're comfortable there. It feels like being home.

In the meantime, do we need to go back to the moon? I'm not sure we do. There is some value in going back. I think the more we discover what the universe is all about, the more people will be convinced that there are probably some intelligent signals floating around out there. If we can capture some, that'd be good. It will confirm what intuitively we probably already know, that there are intelligent beings out there. But the distances are so great and the signals are going to be so faint that it's going to take a huge radio telescope. That's why, I think, if we go back to the moon, one of the really good things we could do is to build a big radio telescope on the back side. It would be fantastic; with no interference from Earth signals, we'd get everything coming in. That means we'd have to set up a lot of other things, such as satellites around the moon to relay communications, but I see that as one nice thing we could do with the moon, if we want to make it useful and go back there.

There might be some things we don't know about the moon that we need to find out. Is there really water ice at its South Pole? If there is, maybe we can use it in some way. But the moon is really beside the point, because the next step needs to be farther out, and we need to develop the capability to do that. Mars is obviously that step. Beyond that, I think there are some other things we can do, but Mars is going to be difficult enough for now.

We're a very young society here. I can imagine another intelligent species out there that's a million years more advanced than us. We think of ourselves as the center of the universe, but there's a universe out there that's billions of years old. It could have intelligent species like us who have been there for a million years and who have figured out all the ways of traveling in space. We will do the same eventually. So to me, there's another logical idea: life may have arrived here from elsewhere in the universe.

If there are other intelligent beings out there, who's to say they didn't go through the same thing we're going through in terms of their sun burning up? That somehow this is connected to life being on this planet? I'm looking at it from the standpoint of the evolutionary business we're in and the prime imperative of everything alive—the survival of the species.

I used to be very careful in talking about that last point. It sounds pretty wild to many people. But I don't care anymore. I really believe I've gotten to a place where I need to say what I want to say. I don't care whether people agree with me or not. I'm simply giving them things to think about.

That got me in a little trouble back in 2017. I was on a morning TV show in England, and they asked me about life out there in the universe. I'd recently been out to Lough Gur in Ireland, a site where people lived comfortably on an island many thousands of years ago. They had a stone circle that started their calendar on the summer solstice every year. I'd been pondering the past. I'm very curious about ancient civilizations. I made some speculative comments I won't go into here, and the British tabloids turned that into something sensational—as they so often do. The truth is that I don't know. I don't have answers. But I like to think about this stuff, because looking out into the universe raised those questions in my mind. I used to be very judicious in sharing my thoughts. Now, who cares?

I've spent almost half a century now sharing my thoughts on spaceflight and encouraging future generations. I'm all too aware that my remaining time trying to promote a spacefaring future is limited. That is why I'm really interested in seeing who is going to take my place.

Back in the 1960s, when I got into this space business, people were leaping into space jobs to help fight the Cold War. It was a matter of national prestige. Now, it feels different. People working in the space industry today want to make humanity better. They believe in their work, because they think our future is not limited to this planet. Personally, I love that.

When it comes to promoting space, I look at folks such as Emily Carney and Amy Teitel. They are young women born long after the Apollo program, and yet they seem to be the biggest fans. They're not reliving old memories when they meet Apollo astronauts. They're discovering history. They write great stuff and really know what they are doing with research. They are personally invested, and when it comes to popularity, they've got a tiger by the tail. They now know all the people from the Apollo era, and they like to be around them. They have fun with it. They are using YouTube and Facebook and other social media in ways that totally bypass the old methods of reaching audiences.

The people I knew during the Apollo program were all absolutely focused on getting to the moon. They would do anything to make the guys happy who were going to fly the missions, but their focus was on getting to the moon. Now the focus is on the guys themselves. People like Amy and Emily are like kids in a candy store when they get talking to us, and they seem to really look up to us. They are both interesting people, which makes the stuff they create fun and interesting too. A lot of their stuff is goofy and irreverent—and funny as hell. I think that's a stroke of genius. I love how this whole new generation are getting into it, in their own unique way. They are a bunch of young, smart people who just think spaceflight is cool, and that is wonderful. It looks like the Apollo program is going to be remembered in ways none of us could have imagined when we were doing it. I love that. I'm grateful to them for sharing our stories.

So after a life of adventure and exploration, where am I now? I'm back in Houston. Back living opposite the space center, in fact. I packed up my home in Michigan in the coldest weather I can remember. To arrive back in warm Houston felt very welcoming.

I'd left Houston under a dark cloud in the early 1970s. I never thought I would come back. That seems like a thousand years ago now. Life can be strange. I have a house in a place that was just swampland half a century ago, when I left. Now, it's pretty upscale. It's a whole new world for me. I think Houston will be okay to me this time around. Besides, the bad guys are no longer here.

I have great friends here. My daughter Alison is just a short drive away. She's a smart kid who has her life sorted out. I'm looking forward to seeing more of her and the family. And there is also good medical care close by—something I have to think about at this time of life. But I'm not stopping. My work with Kallman Worldwide on the Al Worden Endeavour Scholarship is only just beginning. The work is similar to what I was doing before when I chaired the Astronaut Scholarship Foundation—we are providing scholarships to bright kids to help them excel in engineering careers. Except, this time, the scholarship is international. I'm flying all over the world, visiting schools and universities, encouraging these students to excel. It suits me perfectly. I'm a restless type. I need to be out there. I can't sit at home.

Maybe I'll see you out there.

Epilogue

FRANCIS FRENCH

Al Worden passed away in his sleep on 18 March 2020, in Houston, after a brief illness. Although restrictions due to the COVID-19 pandemic prevented all but a very small number of people from being with him during his last days, he was able to enjoy some visits from fellow astronauts, family, and lifelong friends. He passed away surrounded by love and care.

Until the last weeks of his life, he remained active, energetic, and keen to continue his scholarship work around the world. He was eighty-eight, but he could never be described as old. Those who worked with him, many of whom were half his age or less, remarked that they could barely keep up with his energy and fast pace. They also noted that his death created an odd mix of emotions: a sense that Al would have appreciated the fact that he never became an "old man," forced to slow down, mixed with a sense that he had been cheated. He had so much more that he wanted to do.

I only knew Al in the last twenty years of his life and shared a number of adventures with him that will remain forever personal and special. At first, I figured I might be meeting someone whose glory days were behind him. I couldn't have been more wrong. Al used every minute of his long, rich life to the fullest.

You know the saying—never meet your heroes. How many of us have ever approached a favorite music or movie idol only to find the experience underwhelming? Al, on the other hand, was everything you could ever hope for in a spacefarer. Each person he encountered felt as though they had made a close friend. Most at home in a loud bar with a corral of companions, Al made everyone feel welcome and included. And I mean everyone. Those socially awkward folks who generally get marginalized? Al remembered their names and gave them a cheery greeting the next time he saw them.

He wasn't going to slow down. At one point, he bought a home in Michigan, on a golf course; he could have relaxed and just played golf every day. Not Al. He was much too restless. He sold the house, moved back to Houston to be near his family, and started traveling the world again. People like him don't retire. He was excited about this book project, clarifying minor factual points right up into those last weeks. I'm only sorry he won't get to hold a copy in his hands.

Test pilots, famously, don't think about death—at least, not their own. In our many years of interviewing, I only once asked Al what he'd choose as an epitaph. I'd found an article where many Apollo astronauts were asked how they would like to be remembered. At first, he responded, "Have to think about that. Not sure I am qualified to write my own epitaph." But after some time went by, he replied, "What an honor to represent the people from Earth."

Orbiting the moon alone for three days, Al looked out at the universe and gained a perspective no human had ever had before. What he experienced in those hours is a glimpse into a wider universe we have only just begun to explore. It will be centuries until most of humanity can even begin to understand in person what he felt.

I think of him when I see the light of the moon, and I thank him for opening the door for us all.

Acknowledgments

The authors would both like to thank the many people who helped with this book.

Space historian Andrew Chaikin dug out and shared his original Al Worden interview notes for his 1994 book *A Man on the Moon*, which helped revive some old memories.

Thanks to Shalene Baxter, Geoffrey Bowman, Colin Burgess, Emily Carney, Michael Cassutt, Chris DiAnconia, Fred Haise, Jim Hansen, David Hitt, Anne Morrell, Dee O'Hara, Jeannie Bassett Robinson, Jason Rubin, Apollo launch team engineer David Shomper, and Karen Bassett Stevenson for answering questions, reading drafts of this book, and making insightful and helpful suggestions.

Angela Joyce transcribed the many days of interviews we undertook for this book, asked helpful additional questions and for clarifications, plus proofread multiple drafts, making the final version immeasurably better. Dayle Kenyon's insights also greatly sharpened the drafts.

Al Worden's poems first appeared in print in *Family Circle* magazine, August 1972, and were printed in greatly expanded form in his book *Hello Earth: Greetings from Endeavour*, published by Nash Publishing in 1974. We are delighted to share never-before-seen drafts with you in this book.

The team at University of Nebraska Press believed in this project and brought comfort to Al Worden's family and friends by their assurances that this project would continue after he passed away. Thanks go to Rob Taylor, Sara Springsteen, Courtney Ochsner, Tish Fobben, Andrea Shahan, and the rest of their team, along with Jeremy Hall for his sensitive copyediting.

Appendix

Poem from the Far Side of the Moon

Al Worden's first published poem appeared in magazine form in the summer of 1972. Titled "Poems from the Far Side of the Moon," it was printed as one long verse. The poem describes two parts of his *Apollo 15* mission—the drama of launch, followed by the quiet, contemplative time he enjoyed flying solo around the moon.

Some elements of this piece ended up in his book of poems *Hello Earth: Greetings from Endeavour* two years later, but in substantially edited and amended form, broken up into elements of many shorter poetic works. Apollo historian Andrew Chaikin has called them "the poetry of a man caught in the lingering pull of another world."

Blast off
Fast off
July moon
Don't swoon
Speed up
Straight up
Lights flash
Controls thrash.

A vibration, a roar
Motion
Shaking, rattling, we lift
Straight up.

Goodbye my friends
You are gone
The whole world has gone
On a trip.

But this must be finished
Faster, faster, can't turn back
Insignificant, I am insignificant
God on my left
Nothing on my right

Lights flash, panel moves,
Floating in nothingness
Then softly, softly, the movement begins again

Push up the switch
And suddenly light everywhere.

Faster, faster but only in numbers
There is no speed
No motion
Where are we?

This is a mistake
Am I the only one who cares
Upside down trying to fall off
The edge of the Earth?

But we must go on
Compelled by God knows what
To find answers
And rocks

And then—nothing
Lights stop, hearts start
In one monstrous moment
We have defied man
We are in orbit.

Quietly, like a night bird
Floating, soaring, wingless
We glide from shore to shore
Ever curving and falling, but
Not quite touching. Never touching!

Here they come in fantastic procession
Sliding in view, each one a lesson
Liebnitz, Ingenii, Bright One, and King.
Each one different, together they ring
Of history past, see in the present
Dreamlike, cream like, this orbiting crescent.

Now I see where I am going and am
Impatient to get there.
What will I see? The wounds of
Ageless strife? The anguish of cooling
And petrifying? The punctures of an
Infinity of collisions?
No healing, or love, or care, or
Compassion.
She is not healed. The scars
Are all there. From Birth. Poor lady
Of the night.
But we love her, and she knows
It full well, for she has been faithful
All these years.

What of planet Earth? Will
She heal her wounds, love her friends,
Have compassion for the hurt and sick?
It would be so easy to let
It all pass. And end up like her!
Dead, lifeless, revolving slowly
For all the world to see.

Life is too precious
To let ego-centered ideas snuff it out.
The moon must teach us. Not only
Of age, and geology, and planets, and
Solar puzzles.
But of life, else we end up like her!

Intelligent, philosophic, technical
Marvel of an age that turns inwards on
Poverty, needy mothers, Vietnam.
Hopeless? Man is inspired to
Reach out in this fashion
Can he possibly be doing it so he
Won't see his own feet stuck in his own mud?

Oh! I know not, yet the light of
Earth still shines on me, so
Far away. Will I really return?
Will this cold, mechanical, technical
Box survive long enough?
Complete darkness enfolds the
Body and the soul.
The next step is out there, stars
Shining like pieces of light.
There is a pattern out there
But so much brilliance,
Even in the darkness I am honored
The light is suspended between
The darkness
Stretching from side to side like
Billowing waves—almost fluttering.
I glide upward, above the waves
Of ocean moon. Staring, observing,
Wondering why
What am I to do? She is forever
Moving just out of reach
I sail on, never touching, but
Watching and wanting to know

The light is blinding, huge, filling
The mind and stopping all thought.
And everything is suddenly right.

Index

In the Outward Odyssey: A People's History of Spaceflight series

Into That Silent Sea: Trailblazers of the Space Era, 1961–1965
Francis French and Colin Burgess
Foreword by Paul Haney

In the Shadow of the Moon: A Challenging Journey to Tranquility, 1965–1969
Francis French and Colin Burgess
Foreword by Walter Cunningham

To a Distant Day: The Rocket Pioneers
Chris Gainor
Foreword by Alfred Worden

Homesteading Space: The Skylab Story
David Hitt, Owen Garriott, and Joe Kerwin
Foreword by Homer Hickam

Ambassadors from Earth: Pioneering Explorations with Unmanned Spacecraft
Jay Gallentine

Footprints in the Dust: The Epic Voyages of Apollo, 1969–1975
Edited by Colin Burgess
Foreword by Richard F. Gordon

Realizing Tomorrow: The Path to Private Spaceflight
Chris Dubbs and Emeline Paat-Dahlstrom
Foreword by Charles D. Walker

The X-15 Rocket Plane: Flying the First Wings into Space
Michelle Evans
Foreword by Joe H. Engle

Wheels Stop: The Tragedies and Triumphs of the Space Shuttle Program, 1986–2011
Rick Houston
Foreword by Jerry Ross

Bold They Rise: The Space Shuttle Early Years, 1972–1986
David Hitt and Heather R. Smith
Foreword by Bob Crippen

Go, Flight! The Unsung Heroes of Mission Control, 1965–1992
Rick Houston and Milt Heflin
Foreword by John Aaron

Infinity Beckoned: Adventuring Through the Inner Solar System, 1969–1989
Jay Gallentine
Foreword by Bobak Ferdowsi

Fallen Astronauts: Heroes Who Died Reaching for the Moon, Revised Edition
Colin Burgess and Kate Doolan with Bert Vis
Foreword by Eugene A. Cernan

Apollo Pilot: The Memoir of Astronaut Donn Eisele
Donn Eisele
Edited and with a foreword by Francis French
Afterword by Susie Eisele Black

Outposts on the Frontier: A Fifty-Year History of Space Stations
Jay Chladek
Foreword by Clayton C. Anderson

Come Fly with Us: NASA's Payload Specialist Program
Melvin Croft and John Youskauskas
Foreword by Don Thomas

Shattered Dreams: The Lost and Canceled Space Missions
Colin Burgess
Foreword by Don Thomas

The Ultimate Engineer: The Remarkable Life of NASA's Visionary Leader George M. Low
Richard Jurek
Foreword by Gerald D. Griffin

Beyond Blue Skies: The Rocket Plane Programs That Led to the Space Age
Chris Petty
Foreword by Dennis R. Jenkins

A Long Voyage to the Moon: The Life of Naval Aviator and Apollo 17
Astronaut Ron Evans
Geoffrey Bowman
Foreword by Jack Lousma

The Light of Earth: Reflections on a Life in Space
Al Worden with Francis French
Foreword by Dee O'Hara